Estranging Novem

Strange and Glorious Happenings

By Angela Teal who is
J. Reese Bradley

For the hopeless.

Table of Contents

Preface

This book has come about as a way to tell in one place what God has done. God has miraculously delivered me from addiction, mental illness, and, most importantly, my abhorrent sin. I have written online and spoken on podcasts about certain parts of the story, but as I believe anyone the Gospel has transformed is compelled to tell how it happened, this was the best way for me.

While it is my pleasure to tell this story, I give a word of warning that while my other five published books are for tweens and teens, this one includes many mature topics, so I have set the recommended age for this book as 16+ (although Amazon only has 18+ as an option) and urge parents to use discernment when allowing their teen to read this testimony.

Also, as I will be discussing at length my experiences with bulimia, obsessive-compulsive disorder, depression, and anxiety, I must make it clear that I am only telling my experiences, and by no means am I a medical professional in any sense of the term. While I do hope that sharing my symptoms and struggles will lead others suffering to help, this book is not intended to be the help. It is only a signpost pointing first to Jesus Christ and then to possible avenues of treatment if you find yourself or a loved one identifying with any of the issues mentioned.

In conclusion, I so appreciate your time reading *Estranging Novem*. I hope this story finds you well, but if it finds you unwell, you are not alone, and there is help to be had.

J.R.B.

Chapter 1
Estranging Novem

Magnus's little bum buzzes ahead of me. My head doesn't hurt anymore—I feel fine. I'm following Magnus to a door—a bright red door. Estranging Novem. A new thing. That's where we are going. To a new thing. I don't know how I know this, but I do. I've never been more confident of anything in my life.

Maggie Prewitt, *Brumbletide and the Queen's Doctor's Story*

Some children never speak a word until they are four years old, but when they do, they speak in full sentences. Some children never walk until they are two years old and then they are off to the races. I feel I didn't walk or talk until thirty-five or so and am only just now getting the hang of it.

Estranging Novum is a term used to describe the strange, mysterious, and novel phenomena in Science Fiction. *Estranging*, meaning singling out, and *novum*, a "new thing." Estranging the novum is an important task that a Science Fiction writer must try to accomplish in their story.

Estranging *Novem* is my misspelling of the term in my children's fantasy series, *Brumbletide*.

I have decided to name this book after my misspelling because, not only has my life been incredibly strange and mysterious at times and even became a New Thing eventually the year that it really began, but Estranging Novem has become my own definition for how what I set out to do was rarely what I did, but God always worked something good out of it. So, where I meant to include *Estranging Novum* in *Brumbletide* to mean that the hidden world was something strange and new to the people of Little Ipswich, my misspelling technically means something like an alienated nine. Strange and mysterious, indeed.

I began writing this book several months ago, but have scrapped that version because one, I simply cannot write a first draft on the computer. The story doesn't flow as well from my brain to keys as it does from my brain to a pencil. Two, this story is not to be told in the order that it was received. Telling a story the way it is supposed to be told is just as important as the story itself.

At the time of writing this page, I am exactly forty-one and four months. I have a loving husband, an intelligent and quirky son, and a talented and sunny daughter who is everyone's best friend. I have a G.E.D. and no college degrees. I received a group fitness certification twelve years ago after failing the test only once. I have failed just about everything in life once, but I failed my learner's license test twice.

I have written and published five middle grade fantasy novels which even those in their glorious typo-ridden grammatically incorrect state I cannot count as an achievement because those emerged from me just like my two children did—God worked a miracle and birthed something through pain.

When I look at my son and my daughter, I see little walking visions of God's glory and craftsmanship. My daughter in particular is a constant reminder that God always knows best no matter how much we think we do—more on that in other chapters. *Brumbletide*, too, is a vision like these. Who knew what would be? Who knew what *could* be?

My two children and five books are the work of God and the work of God alone. The proof is in my constant failures throughout my life thus far, and whatever good comes from my life hereafter will be God's doing and God's doing alone. Many people reply to this with "You don't give yourself enough credit" or something similar, but it is true, and I will prove it to you by giving an account of what has happened. And that is what this book is, an account of what has happened. It is not meant to teach, persuade, therapize, or impose though it will probably seem like it at times. This is the true story of bizarre and glorious happenings in the life of a woman who lived a sinful life and was then radically rescued and changed by the Gospel of Jesus Christ.

Soli Deo Gloria. Glory to God alone.

This is the story of my Estranging Novem which was mostly strange, confusing, and chaotic until God brought about His Estranging Novum that changed everything, and because of this I have resolved to die on the hill of Christianity. Of course, what are our promises to God? Nothing. The only promises that hold any weight are His promises to us. We can only lay our resolutions at His feet and pray for Him to establish them.

I have also resolved to live a life of writing books that most may never read in a more and more technological and artificially intelligent world. I have resolved to continue to write even though I risk being out of touch with the generation I am writing for. This comes after decades of self-imposed turmoil that you will read about here. I have done nothing right so far—all the right that has happened has been from the hand of God Himself. If you do not believe me, if this sounds dramatic, be sure to read the rest of this book. I was not only dead before, but I was some zombie-like creature, walking though dead and feeding off others. Truly, I was not alive until God gave my life through Christ Jesus.

I have been crucified with Christ. It is no longer I who live but Christ in me. And the life I now live in the flesh I live by faith in the Son of God, who loved me and gave Himself for me. Galatians 2:20

Through Jesus, God has not only made a New Creation, but has also miraculously worked together for good my wrongdoing, foolishness, and failures time and time again.

Here is how it went.

Chapter 2
The Precious Trunchbull

When she marched—Miss Trunchbull never walked, she always marched like a storm-trooper with long strides and arms swinging—when she marched along a corridor you could actually hear her snorting as she went, and if a group of children happened to be in her path, she ploughed right on through them like a tank, with small people bouncing off to her left and right. Thank goodness, we don't meet many people like her in this world, although they do exist and all of us are likely to come across at least one of them in a lifetime.

Roald Dahl, *Matilda*

My earliest memory is of standing outside at night at the house on Romulus in our neighborhood of Centurion Hills with my dad, whom I adored. He was smoking a cigarette. I was looking at the stars and the ground around his feet. I was very close to his feet back then.

Maybe I came up with this memory on my own. I have several of those, I'm sure. But I think this one did happen. I have another memory of performing for my dad on the fireplace hearth with a Yogi Bear taller than I was. I'm not sure which came first, the night outside or the Yogi Bear, but I do know that I would go on to be taller than both Yogi and my dad, and it was these years before my little brother was born when all the attention was on me, that I was the least sinful I would ever be. To the naked eye, I was sweet and innocent and good, but on the inside, I was a precious little Trunchbull.

Agatha Trunchbull was the hideous headmaster of Crunchem Hall Primary School in Roald Dahl's *Matilda*. She hated children, loved only herself, and anyone that got in her way she threw in the Chokey, which was an upright coffin with nails inside.

I am my father's firstborn, my mother's thirdborn, the only girl, and somehow still managed to live like an only child. I have two older half-brothers I thought were pure magic. I loved them, and they loved me, probably due to them being five and ten years older than me and especially the fact that we didn't see each other very much because they visited every other weekend. They played sports and had skateboards and nun-chucks and cool magazines. Jimmy and Eric were celebrities in my eyes.

My first opportunity to display wickedness was when my full-blood baby brother, Walt, was born. I hated him from the minute I saw him. And I really hated him. Amazingly, we marvel at Cain killing Abel because of jealousy when there are siblings all over the world displaying the same kind of behavior, and naturally at that. No one teaches these little beasts to be wicked. No one taught me. I had a natural indwelling hatred for my brother from the moment he came into the world and treated him wickedly until we were teenagers.

Both of our parents worked hard at their jobs to support the household. But this meant Walt and I were latch-key kids in the early 90s, and with our parents not around to watch, I would beat, bite, and torment Walt just for being him. I was horrible, and I know that was damaging to him, even in the long run. Why do we laugh at siblings abusing siblings? It is real abuse and nothing short of wicked.

But while Walt did nothing to deserve the harm dealt, I never *tried* to be abusive. It was nothing I saw on television. My parents rarely fought. No one taught me how to hate. It was already in me and only grew as I grew. Sure, I became more mature as I aged, but the sin in my heart also grew and morphed into adult, mature sin that knew well how to manipulate. I lied to others, and the sin lied to me.

Still, I thought of myself as a good person. No matter my actions, to me, I was always that good girl checking out Dad's feet and performing with Yogi Bear. Walt would yell, "Everyone thinks you're nice, but you're not! I know how you really are!" And he was right.

To our parents and everyone else, I was kind, sweet, and bubbly. To my friends, I was extremely submissive, an *"I don't care, what do you want you want to do?"* kind of friend. From adults, I constantly received compliments about how well-behaved I was and, later, even how wise and level-headed I was for my age. But the real you is who you are when no one is looking. And the real me was wicked.

When we were teenagers, Walt and I finally became friends. He understandably had a chip on his shoulder toward me and would occasionally give me a good kick or punch, but for the most part, we had become friends, and my hatred shifted toward my underserving mother.

My parents got divorced when I was fifteen, and after that, I didn't see my father for two years. I'm not sure why this was; I have a theory about children and fathers that I won't explain because I am no psychologist, but even though Mom was the disciplinarian of the two, when Dad was gone, I wasn't at all afraid of my mother. I became viciously rebellious, sneaking out at night, smoking cigarettes in my room, and saying the nastiest things to her, among other terrible doings. How she didn't send me away, I'll never know. There was probably no place to send me.

Still, all through abusing my brother and mother, in my mind, I always had a good reason for acting the way I did. There were *real* bad people out there, and then there was me, not a bad person, but having reasons to be bad in these cases because of the hand I had been dealt.

I also had the idea that if I didn't get caught and didn't think about it for long, my crime didn't happen. I wasn't a thief or a liar as long as no one knew. And, of course, I wasn't really a thief and a liar anyway. Those were out there somewhere, but they were not me. I had reasons.

At the age of seventeen, the story I told myself and everyone else when I dropped out of school and moved out of my house was that I left an abusive, chaotic household to brave the world all on my own. Our family was dysfunctional, this was true, but my actions stemmed from no other place than my own black heart.

So there I was, selfish, narcissistic, lazy, and entitled. The girl everyone had told was so wise for her age made the brilliant decision to drop out of school, leave home, and take on the great, wide world, enrolling in the school of Hard Knocks. I remember actually thinking these words to myself: *I know all there is to know. There is nothing else I need to learn.*

Ha!

What a mess I was mentally, physically, and, most of all, spiritually. But God's grace is truly amazing as the song says. Though I fell on my face and through the mud time and time again, God, in His great mercy, would one day rescue me from it all and even use my myriad of mistakes for good.

God would, indeed, rescue me and make good of everything. But that was well in the future.

Chapter 3
Peter Pan

J.M. Barrie, *Peter Pan*

Some of you will remember this scene from *Brumbletide and the Daughter of Eve*. It really happened.

"Where are you going?"

"Home."

"You're not going anywhere. You've made our lives a living hell for a week, leaving this place a total mess!"

The above is not written in italics because it is not the excerpt from *Brumbletide* when Maggie was kept at Nan's Pancakes for not finishing her work. This was the actual exchange between a first-shift Waffle House waitress and my seventeen-year-old self.

I had dropped out of high school and left home. I wasn't old enough yet to work in a restaurant that served alcohol, so I planned on working at Waffle House, a twenty-four-hour breakfast restaurant, for six months until I could get a job at a finer dining establishment. A week into working the overnight shift, an annoyed first-shift waitress reamed me a new one for leaving them with dirty floors, dirty bathrooms, smudged windows, and dishes in the dish pit for five mornings straight. I am sure that during my training week these duties were explained and even shown to me. I probably even performed them. But while I am not an expert in much, I am an expert in not paying attention, especially when I was seventeen. I did wonder a few times during my shifts who they had hired to sweep and clean the windows and things. It was me!

The first-shift waitress accosting me after my ten-hour overnight shift was the nail in the Waffle coffin. My spoiled, entitled, lazy self had already been planning its permanent exit, and today was the day! I would never return to Waffle House in my life.

Two factors foiled my plan. One, I was terrified of confrontation, and two, the little Waffle House manager, Samantha, was not terrified of confrontation at all.

The next night that I was scheduled to go in, I didn't. When I didn't show up, Samantha called and called and called and called and called. And called.

And called.

I did not answer the phone. I planned to never return to that Waffle House again in my life, maybe not even that area of town. Maybe I would never go to any Waffle House restaurant ever again just for good measure.

When I did not answer her nine hundred calls, the woman showed up at the apartment where I was staying and told me to get dressed and that she was going to drive me to work.

I was shocked. I got dressed, got in Samantha's car, and she drove us to Waffle House, where I worked for six years.

I hated Waffle House with every fiber of my being—but I loved it too. It was hard work, and I found myself in many sketchy predicaments. It may be different these days, but Waffle House used to have a reputation for hiring anything with a pulse. If someone couldn't get a job, they could always get hired at Waffle House even if they had been fired from there before. On any given shift, you (likely a degenerate yourself—I was) will be working with drug addicts, former prostitutes, thieves, or just flat out crazy people. As I write this, I am reminded of working second shift alone with Jim Rainbolt, who was at the time under investigation for the murder of his wife, Emilie. I would make friends with co-workers my age; we would get to know each other pretty well, I thought, but the next thing I knew, they were in jail for drugs or stealing.

I would use the common saying here, "There were all walks of life," but there were not. It was mostly the dregs of society of which I was the worst. Somehow, miraculously, I never got into drugs, and I don't remember stealing anything from that particular job, but where I took the prize for "the worst" was that

I was miserable to work with. In my mind, like Peter Pan, I was "the one." Everyone else had to grow up, but not me. I had opted out. But I also expected everyone to stop what they were doing and help me when I wanted them to. And now that I'm thinking about it, I did steal! A woman and her kids came into the Waffle House I was working at in Norcross. She gave me a sad story about how they didn't have any money or food. She lucked out that the waitress working was young and naïve, because I believed her and gave her a ton of food! The cook, who makes a bonus from shift sales, told the manager, and I got in trouble. I was no angel, as I've gone into already, but in this case, I thought surely the management would have done the same thing for this poor woman. That turned out not to be the case, but I didn't get fired. A classic Waffle House scenario!

The cook that lost his bonus was by far not my only enemy, and for good reason. As it turned out, the girl who was told—and, in turn, believed—she was wise and level-headed for her age, when put under the least little bit of pressure, lost her ever-living mind, throwing full-on tantrums and crying like a baby. At that point in my life, I had zero work ethic. I made each shift miserable for any server scheduled with me because I was lazy and would lose my temper, even throwing things and kicking doors when I got overwhelmed during busy times. All of the drug addicts, thieves, and psychos worked hard and did not complain. Not me. I was the most cringe-worthy worst. But although it was hard on everyone else, Waffle House was exactly what I needed.

I thank God all the time that the waitress ripped into me that morning, and that Samantha came to get me that night. No other place would have allowed me to stay on as an employee acting the way I did. But I was able to stay an employee at Waffle House even though I was the precious Trunchbull that I was, and eventually, I calmed down quite a bit and actually came to enjoy hard work.

My favorite God-send at Waffle House was Terri Lynn. She was two years older than me, married already, and had a motherly nature about her. We became good friends, and Terri took me under her wing, keeping me out of so much trouble I would have certainly gotten myself into. Not to say I didn't get into trouble. I did. But thanks to Terri, I am still alive and never became a crack-addicted prostitute.

Of all things, strangely, Waffle House, through the years, became a place of comfort. When my life was extra chaotic, a Waffle House shift was always waiting, granting me a nice dose of familiarity and accomplishment to make me feel like I might actually be able to make it on my own, whether that was true or not. I not only learned work ethic and the way of the real world, but I learned so much from the customers as well. I served celebrities and average Joes, professors and students, fit people and the morbidly obese, doctors and psychopaths—who were sometimes the same person. I think I even waited on a demon a few times. He would leave me marijuana as a tip and tell me he wanted my heart, soul, and mind. And, of course, he probably wasn't the only demon.

I watched parents serve their children and try to teach them to order for themselves. I saw friendly people I knew outside of Waffle House treat the waitstaff like slaves. I saw drug deals and prostitutes. I learned the culture of nightclub employees, the culture of the daytime workforce, and the culture of the elderly. Teenagers my own age tried to get me to let them buy cigarettes from the cigarette machine. I let them until I realized they would then sit at my tables, never order anything, and in the rare case they did, they didn't tip.

Interestingly, I got to where I could guess correctly what someone would order just by looking at them.

Young and old, rich and poor, wise and ignorant, every race and culture, every walk of life, I served them all and learned something from everyone. It was the rocky terrain of the school of Hard Knocks, but it was certainly teaching me.

Even if I had never dropped out of high school and run away, I often wonder where my work ethic would have come from. At home, I had fallen too far behind to graduate. College was out of the question. Mom was too busy trying to fix everything that had gone wrong to worry about what I was doing. Thank God the first-shift waitress yelled at me. Thank God Samantha came to get me. Thank God Terri Lynn took me under her wing and was such a good friend. Thank God for waitressing, and thank God for Waffle House.

Chapter 4
Two Egg Whites
'N a Cup of Coffee

"I cannot be right all the time. Quite often I is left instead of right."
Roald Dahl, *The BFG*

Dark times are ahead. Let's hear a funny story first! Third shift, or the graveyard shift as some call it, at Waffle House is the overnight shift that starts at 9:00 p.m. and ends at 7:00 a.m. There is something so depressing about the sun coming up, people getting breakfast and getting their day started, and you going home to bed. But I digress.

I was seventeen and not used to staying up all night. A man walked in one night, sat at the high counter, and quickly told me he would like "Two egg whites 'n a cup of coffee."

"You got it," I replied. Lucky for him, my mom's roommate had *just* told me that day about what she called "shepherd's coffee," where an egg white is dropped into the coffee to remove the bitterness. Today was his day! What were the odds that someone would order shepherd's coffee that very night?

I poured a cup of coffee, took it to the Egyptian cook who spoke little English, and after some confused arguing, finally got him to drop two egg whites into the cup. I proudly brought the man his shepherd's coffee that he didn't even have to explain what it was.

The man looked at the mug as if he couldn't quite put together what he was seeing—and then burst out laughing.

You guessed it. He had ordered two egg whites *and* a cup of coffee.

Chapter 5
Demented

"Dementors are among the foulest creatures that walk this earth. They infest the darkest, filthiest places, they glory in decay and despair, they drain peace, hope, and happiness out of the air around them. Even Muggles feel their presence, though they can't see them. Get too near a Dementor and every good feeling, every happy memory will be sucked out of you. If it can, the Dementor will feed on you long enough to reduce you to something like itself ...soul-less and evil. You'll be left with nothing but the worst experiences of your life."

J.K. Rowling, *Harry Potter and the Prisoner of Azkaban*

When I was eleven and twelve, I had a group of friends in the neighborhood. We were very Old School in the way we were, a real-life *Sandlot*. We were together every day, playing outside until the street lights came on, or we would rollerblade in our friend Chrissy's basement when it rained. Holding hands, we would skateboard down the big hills in our neighborhood. We'd ride bikes, go on adventures, and do all of the things 80s kids say they did even though we were 90s kids.

In our group was Brian, Alex, Chrissy, Courtney, Ali, and me. Chrissy and Courtney were next-door neighbors, Ali and Alex lived close by each other, and Brian lived right behind my house. Our yards connected.

My parents lived in the house on Romulus Drive when I was born and moved literally around the corner when I was four to Augustus Drive. Brian lived behind me there. When I was five or so, my dad built a fantastic treehouse for me in the backyard. I was up there one day when Brian was in his yard and asked him to come play in it. He jumped the fence and climbed up. We had a great time! That is until my dog came outside. What Brian didn't know, and what I had forgotten, was that our family rottweiler, Lady, was extremely fun-loving—unless you jumped the fence. A water meter reader had jumped the fence once and hit her with a stick. She was jaded about it ever since. Lady would not let Brian come down out of the treehouse. We stayed up there until it was dark, and our parents finally came to help.

Fast-forward to middle school, when Brian and I were part of the neighborhood crew that hung out on the one flat road in our neighborhood, which we called the Flat Top. We all had different lives at school, but in the neighborhood, we were best friends.

Brian was the oldest of us, and I don't think any of us knew then that he was the glue that held us all together until we did know.

I had gone out to the store with Mom one afternoon, and when we pulled up in our driveway coming home, there were ambulances and firetrucks in front of Brian's house and a crowd of first responders in his yard huddled around something.

Brian had been working for one of our other neighbors and rode to and from work with him every day. Brian's backyard and my backyard connected, but while the street in front of my house was a quiet neighborhood street where the speed limit was twenty-five, in front of Brian's house was a busy, winding road. When Brian got out of the van and stepped onto Old Peachtree Road, a speeding car hit him into his yard, where he died. He was fifteen and would have been sixteen the next day. The fact that he died so close to his birthday made it worse somehow.

When Mom finally told me that Brian had died, I had been waiting anxiously to hear. Nothing like that had ever happened before to anyone I'd known. When the final verdict came, I went upstairs to my room—and laughed.

I don't know why I laughed! I wasn't happy. I was shocked. I think it was some weird anxiety response. But I felt horrible about that for years.

Then I went numb. The neighborhood crew went to Brian's funeral. It was open casket. There he was, looking nothing like himself. His face was flat, eyes glued shut. The whole thing was so strange. I didn't cry. While all my friends were crying, I couldn't even *make* myself cry. Courtney and Chrissy gave a lovely speech about Brian and our group. They cried the whole time. There I sat. Stunned.

I finally cried that Sunday. I had gone to Sunday School at church. Our teacher sat in the little room with a circle of chairs. No one else had come yet. I sat down beside her, and of all things, she said, "Did you hear about that boy who was hit and killed by a car this week?" She had no clue he was my friend. For some strange reason it was then the waterworks came. Not long after Brian's death, while most of us remained friends, the neighborhood crew no longer got together on the Flat Top.

Death certainly left its mark on the neighborhood of Centurion Hills. Brian was by far not the only early death. Almost every house on our circle had someone that died an untimely death. I thought that my house had escaped the fate until I remembered that a girl who lived in our house before us had drowned at four years old!

I vividly remember playing at one house with the little sister of a boy who had died at only eighteen not long before. Her parents were fighting, and the dad yelled, "I miss him too!"

It was sad that the boy had died young, but I learned then that death was the worst for those left behind. They had to continue on living, reeling in the pain and agony of loss.

I tell you all this because I was constantly anxious and scared as a kid for seemingly no reason, but I think this contributed to it along with another story I will tell you in the next chapter. Everything seemed like it was going to end at any given moment. Every time I loved someone or something, I felt deep sadness at the same time knowing I couldn't trust that they would last. I couldn't get too attached. But, of course, you do find yourself getting attached to things and people, and the more attached I was, the sadder and more anxious I became.

I didn't realize it until decades later, but this fear and anxiety that had shrouded me at such a young age was the fertilizer and rain for the thorny thicket that would become my life. The thorns would prick not only me but many others, causing a bloody mess.

Chapter 6
Little Ipswich Will End?

"Hey, Mum?"

"Make it quick. You know my show's on in a few minutes."

"What was that movie you guys were watching about?"

Mum huffs—but then grins. My stomach twists. In case you weren't able to read between the lines of my sarcasm, my mother is a selfish, lazy gossip who strangely finds joy in the misery of others. By the twinkle in her eye, I know that what she is about to tell me is something horrible because horrible is her favorite kind of news to deliver.

"Yes, dear!" She is sickeningly sweet. "That particular movie happens to be based on a real prophecy from Pippin's Puzzle." She eyes me for any hint of fear. I refuse to give it to her even though I'm definitely on edge. We aren't Batch-goers, but some of the families in the neighborhood are. I know that Pippin's Puzzle is a book about someone named, well, Pippin. The book is highly respected even by non-Batch-goers. We've learned about Pippin's Puzzle at school, and I've gathered bits and pieces over the years about a gathering called Batch held at Emily. Little Ipswich is an otherwise average small town except for Emily, an enormous stone castle set afloat in the Lux Sea that borders us. While I have never been, I know that anyone can go to Batch, and it also has its own school inside that one of our neighbors, Atticus Peabody, attends.

"The prophecy is true, Mags," Mum says urgently.

"I know." I didn't know.

"It's from the twenty-first book of Pippin's Puzzle. It tells of how one day, life here in Little Ipswich will end." She pauses, waiting for my reaction. What mother does this? "There will be seven years of unspeakable anguish for all who live here at the time." Her eyes narrow and her voice is melancholy. "Dark times, dark times indeed. Hold on, let me find it!"

J. Reese Bradley, *Brumbletide and the Daughter of Eve*

I spent many years sick to my stomach with fear, thinking it was the end of the world, which made me fearful of church, the Bible, and Christianity as a whole. Before telling this true story, it is important to know that Margerie Prewitt, the terrible mother from *Brumbletide*, is not at all like my own mother. Margerie was a fun (for me) creation inspired by Roald Dahl's over-the-top villains. That said, this scene from *Brumbletide and the Daughter of Eve* was based on real life.

I was seven or eight years old, and my parents were watching *The Omen* during dinner. *The Omen* is a horror movie about the antichrist. We did eat in the living room like the Prewitts. Just like Maggie, I couldn't figure out what was going on in the plot, but it gave me the creeps. When it was over, I asked my mom what it was about, and she opened the Bible to the book of Revelation and read parts of it while explaining to me that *The Omen* was based on this very true prophecy!

I was so scared I was sick and had nightmares for *years*. Years! I was always waiting for the sky to unzip, Jesus to descend out of it, and the world to come to a cataclysmic end at any moment. To make matters all the worse, I saw signs everywhere that it would happen soon.

I went to church because I had a fear of God, but I didn't like it, and I especially didn't like going at night. I once went with my friend, Anastasia, to Vacation Bible School at her church. It was fun for everyone except me. We would go from station to station where the teachers talked about different Bible stories. One station was about the Exodus, one of my favorite Bible stories now as an adult, but I was terrified by the "angel of death" smoke that ominously drifted past the doorway from a hidden bucket of dry ice.

At the end of that week, all of us kids sat in the sanctuary in the dark and watched the massive choir dressed in white robes act out the rapture and the end of the world. I closed my eyes and plugged my ears with my fingers. I did *not* want to see it. I couldn't understand why everyone was celebrating the end of the world and possibly never seeing their family or friends again. Also, there was the not-so-small detail that Jesus would come without warning like a "thief in the night," so we needed to be ready at all times. As a ten-year-old, I found myself in a lot of sticky situations. What if I was in one of those when Jesus came back? What if I didn't go? I had been told those left behind would receive a mark of 666 on their hand and forehead. I constantly checked.

This is funny now, but it was not at all funny as a kid living it. I would wake up sweating in the middle of the night and throw up out of sheer terror. Whenever there was an outdoor event, especially at night and at a place where the open sky was visible, I was haunted that the stars would fall, and the moon would turn to blood at any minute. I currently hold a preterist view of eschatology, and I am sure this is why.

If what Mom had told me was true, why was everyone looking forward to it? Not to mention the years of terrible tribulation where Christians would be murdered for their faith, all before the grand finale of the world coming to a fiery end. Jesus would then erupt out of the sky, and all of us would leave our lives as we knew them to rise up into the air where we would live who knows where for *eternity. Eternity.*

This fear followed me everywhere I went for most of my life. The thing about fear is that if you are scared, you believe in at least some part of what you are fearful about. I didn't love God, I didn't want to do what He said, and I didn't want to let go of my idols, but I believed in Him.

Both this crippling fear and this belief in God are significant players in the story ahead. But the crippling fear would be a symptom of something that would take me down multiple decades of darkness and shame.

Many are suffering the same thing and have no idea.

Chapter 7
Shaggy Maggie

My brown mop-like hair, gap in my oversized teeth, and charity shop wardrobe do not help my reputation at school. I don't have any friends. I don't mind being alone and even prefer it except when there is a school trip or dance. Then it is blatantly apparent that I am friendless, and the odds of getting bullied are much higher. Tom Schafer is usually the one up to the job getting the class to chant "Shaggy Maggie" or "Maggie is a rabbit," so cleverly making fun of my teeth. However, today, I'm so excited that I feel almost pretty in my pink floral dress. The pit in my stomach from the doomsday news is, for the moment, replaced with butterflies for a new adventure. Maybe I will even make a friend at the castle today. Probably not, but maybe.

Maggie Prewitt, *Brumbletide and the Daughter of Eve*

It was my fourteenth birthday. I was in eighth grade. Duluth Middle School had outgrown itself, so Richard Hull Middle was built, and I was rezoned to it. With the split, my already small friends group got even smaller. I had two friends that I ate lunch with every day, Blair and Rachel. My birthday is December 20th and was usually the last day before Christmas break. On this particular birthday, Blair and Rachel left for vacation early, leaving me sitting alone at lunch. I sat in the same spot we always sat; just today, I was by myself, which I guess is what made the space appealing to a bully, who we will call Bully Riggins for this story.

Before I go on, let me say that I am Bully Riggins in the story of others. I have been a horrible person many times, and much worse than this Bully Riggins was to me. I am only including this part of the story because it is important to the plot. It was the first domino that fell. I have pushed many dominos—this is not about Bully Riggins. It is about the beginning of my tumultuous journey with bulimia nervosa.

Seeing I was alone surrounded by several empty seats, Bully Riggins and his posse—yes, posse—lumbered over and stood with their lunch trays, sulking at me like I was a flat tire. Then, like out of a movie, Bully Riggings harshly told me to move because he and his gang wanted to sit at that end of the table. Startled, I looked around the busy lunchroom for another place to sit, but when I didn't move fast enough, Bully began loudly berating and insulting me to move. The rowdy lunchroom then quieted down to see what was going on.

I was humiliated to the point that the room started to spin. As I sat in my stunned stupor, from out of nowhere, like a magical unicorn, swooped in a beautiful cheerleader. She was popular and didn't usually say much to me, but she yelled at the boys to leave me alone and then sat and ate with me the rest of the time. She was lovely.

I was ruined.

My son and I recently attended the Rising Sixth Graders Night at the middle school. The counselors met with us all first and explained to us that little things to adults are big things to middle schoolers. I can attest that this is true. Of course, now this incident seems silly, but back then, I was ruined.

The cheerleader sat with me, trying to act normal, while I cried. I couldn't stop crying the rest of the day. My teacher took me out in the hall to ask what happened. I couldn't tell her. I was so embarrassed. I never wanted to come back to school again—and I wouldn't. After that day, I would be different.

I went home. I lost nine pounds over Christmas break. I started exercising and wearing makeup. And this was the beginning of a twenty-year battle with bulimia.

That seems rather much, doesn't it? Did one incident with Bully Riggins really cause twenty years of bulimia? No. Bulimia happened to be a symptom of something already inside of me that was kickstarted and then propelled and made worse with the direction my life would go. Bulimia and obsessive-compulsive disorder will be discussed in full in later chapters, but at that point in my life, I didn't know I had either of those, and it was this trauma event to my eighth-grade OCD brain that got the ball of disorder rolling.

When I returned to school in January, everyone showered me with compliments on my transformation, and people who had never said two words to me before were now noticing me and being friendly at that. To an ordered mind, this is where it would stop, but not for a disordered mind. From then on, I was consumed with weight, exercise, and my physical appearance. My Bible was Cosmopolitan Magazine, which I read religiously. I did pray, but I prayed every night for God to help me stick to my exercise and dieting and always to help me lose weight. I lived only to be thin and beautiful. This was obviously a terrible mindset, but it became my *only* mindset as the days went on.

My parents divorced two years later in a not at all peaceful way. That caused not only the family to fall apart but every one of us to fall apart individually as well. The eating disorder went from bad to worse and then even worse when new roommates moved in with my mother.

I didn't realize it back then, and even if I had, I wouldn't have known why, but the bulimia had and would continue to worsen with each big change that happened.

With the eating disorder raging and my home life dilapidated, my already unfocused mind was now entirely distracted from the schoolwork I struggled with anyway. In April of 1999 (I think), with it obvious I would not be moving on to the next grade level—again, I made the impulsive decision to quit school and run away from home. I packed some things, left my mom a note that I had moved out, moved in with a girl from my homeroom class, and got a nightshift job at Waffle House.

Even after enrolling in the School of Hard Knocks, I was still bulimic and still striving for approval from anything that breathed. I was still trying to be this beautiful specimen for the world, even in a breakfast-colored uniform and head scarf. The disordered thinking didn't end any time soon after leaving home and dropping out, and I eventually got a job at Hooters. It is probably difficult to read this part without laughing. Know I am laughing with you. Hooters is a sports bar where the girls wear tiny, tight shorts and tank tops, and a large part of the job is to be beautiful. My thinking was that this job would *force* me to stay thin and pretty, and if I was actually hired, that meant that I was, in fact, at least pretty enough to be a Hooters girl.

"Again, you're okay with the uniform?" the manager asked me.

"Yes," I replied.

"What size?"

"Medium."

"Don't say curse words like that. Small, extra small, or extra extra small?"

"Small, please."

He was joking, but those really were the sizes, and I was going to at least fit into an extra small before my time there was done.

As with Waffle House, I had a love/hate relationship with Hooters. When I wasn't throwing up, I felt like the fattest waitress there, and when I was, I felt like I belonged but was always at death's door.

I would get up some days and decide not to go to work like I did all of my other jobs. In these kinds of jobs, you can do that and not get fired until after you've done it several times. Again, Peter Pan. In my mind, I was always "the one" that it was fine to do what shouldn't be done. This attitude of "the one" would come to bite me badly.

Being one of the beautiful girls, even if by name tag only, and getting so much attention from men was enough to keep me coming back to work. I moved in with two of the waitresses I worked with, making sure I paid extra for the master bedroom so that I could hide the bingeing and purging the best I could. I was also dating my ex-husband at this time—more on that to come.

I stayed at Hooters for a few years until one of our most popular waitresses got fired and began waitressing at a strip club in Atlanta. As it turned out, this marked the beginning of another significant change in my life. As you may have noticed, almost none of the changes so far in my twenty-something years on the earth were for the better. This one wasn't either.

Chapter 8
Narcissus

"May he who loves not others love himself."
Prayer from a rejected admirer in
Hamilton's Mythology

Many people with pasts like mine say, "I wouldn't change a thing because I wouldn't be the person I am now without it all."

I would change most of it.

Thankfully, the story gets *much* better down the line, but if I could, I would change so much. If I had come to know God before making all of the poor decisions I did, He would still have given me New Life in Him. He would still have refined me and grown me. It would have still been a wonderful, I would say even better, testimony. But this is what happened, and it is hopefully a warning story to you who are young about what happens when you do not know God early in life, even if you think you do. He brings so much beauty from the ashes that result from burning your life to the ground. But, dear reader, if you haven't already set everything on fire, save yourself so much anguish and turmoil by calling out to God now, "Dear God, I need you! I don't even know why, but please come save me!"

What seems romantic, edgy, and exciting from the outside is nothing but a coffin on the inside, a place for the dead.

Greek Mythology's Narcissus fell in love with his own reflection in the waters of a spring and ended up killing himself because he could not have his object of desire. Narcissus flowers sprung up where he died. December is the month in which I was born, and the Narcissus is its flower. Fitting.

I am including this part of the story because, for one thing, I am so far removed from it that no one could possibly imagine me doing this anymore. Two, it is truly incomprehensible how blinding sin can be, so I am hoping to spell it out here through the story of my actions. Believe it or not, I actually did all of this while calling myself a Christian and saying my prayers at night.

When the Hooters girl got the waitressing job at the strip club called Pink Pony, word got around that she was making a killing. Irresponsible with everything at the time, money was no exception. The idea that I could make a lot of money was enticing, and I was curious to see what actually went on in strip clubs anyway. Not to mention, the women were beautiful as I wanted to be.

I was the second of the Hooters girls to switch to Pink Pony. I can't remember how this all worked out, but I had a friend from the neighborhood I grew up in who also waitressed at the club already. I remember calling her and asking about it. I was so nervous. It felt like I was crossing a line like Michelle talks about in *Rise of the Firebreather*. I wanted to cross it; I just didn't want anyone in my life to know I crossed it. I went up to the club one night, walked into the ticket area, and told the woman behind the counter why I was there. The manager came out and was very straight to the point about how I needed to get a permit and when I should come back. I got the permit and then got the job as a cocktail waitress.

Early on, I pulled my usual no-show shenanigans, calling and saying I couldn't make it to work. That didn't fly like it had everywhere else. The manager that gave me the job yelled over the phone about how I had made a commitment, and I could come in or not come back.

Waitressing at the strip club was so stressful. You had to run to catch customers before the other waitresses so the patrons would start a bar tab with you. I do not have a competitive bone in my body, so this was difficult. After you have marked your customers, you then serve them drinks all night all the while urging them to get a V.I.P. room. A V.I.P. room is where customers can be somewhat one-on-one with the dancer of their choice—and it costs a lot of money. This was supposed to be good for both the dancer and the waitress because we waitresses were supposed to be tipped on the total cost of the room. So if the dancer is paid $3,000, the waitress is supposed to tell the patron that it is customary to tip the waitress twenty percent of the total cost, which would be $600. Many waitresses were excellent at smooth-talking this kind of tip out of the men. I, on the other hand, nervously tried to explain this to the customer and usually ended up talking him out of tipping me anything at all. After a while, I just started adding the twenty percent tip without asking, which worked about half the time and caused a slurry huff from the drunken patron the other half.

Meanwhile, the dancers were treated like royalty. They were worshipped, catered to, and no one bothered questioning them on how much they cost. In fact, I watched on as men literally *threw* money at them! They were gorgeous, and many of them lived fabulous lives outside of the club. I had always heard about strip clubs being places where washed-up women with no other choice in life went to support their drug habit or prostitute themselves. If that was going on, I didn't see it. However, I did see women get fired. The rules at this club, in particular, were very strict, which now I see was a gift from God. Anyone caught doing drugs or having any intimate contact of any kind with customers, even in the V.I.P. rooms, was fired immediately. For the most part, these women were not anything like what I had heard. They were not only unspeakably beautiful but were making six-figure incomes while in law school and medical school. Many saved their money and paid cash for their homes and luxury vehicles. Also, a lot of them had husbands and kids, which, to this day, I don't know how that worked.

Needless to say, it didn't take long for me to ditch waitressing for a pair of platforms. Now, remember, the most important thing to me was being beautiful, and in my spiritually blind state, I had found the answer to all of my problems. I finally wasn't struggling financially, but for me, even though it was nice not having to worry about how the bills would be paid, more than anything, the money meant that I was *worth* paying for. I was admired and sought after. I could ask for anything I wanted and easily get it. In my mind, I had finally reached the mountain top.

But as God would have it, the two times I became a dancer, something got in the way shortly after. The ex-husband, who wasn't even a husband yet, asked me to marry him. Afraid of any confrontation, I wasn't brave enough to say no, and I quit dancing when we got married.

I convinced myself that the marriage would be good for me, another thing to force me to stay in shape and beautiful and also keep me on top of my finances. He was very strict with fitness and money, and it had been made clear that I had to be as well.

Heed my warning. When two narcissistic, mentally ill, unrepentant sinners decide to marry, it is survival of the fittest.

I was not the fittest.

All of the fire I had been playing with for years was about to finally burn me. We had a beautiful wedding. All of my family and the friends he deemed worthy came. We had a glorious honeymoon. When we came home from Aruba, his mother was at the house, and those two were the married ones for the duration of the marriage. Some sort of third-wheel roommate, I was alone and trapped.

I got a job at Starbucks, which I began right after the honeymoon. All of the money I made went into his hands and was off-limits to me. Life there was very regimented. I was isolated from friends and family and was only allowed to be at the house, Starbucks, and the gym without special permission. It was a mistake on his part to allow me to go to the gym. It would end up being my way out.

That marriage lasted five miserable years. Two or so were spent trying to make it work; the rest of the time was spent planning my escape back to exotic dancing, where I was someone.

Chapter 9
Bruce Bogtrotter

The Trunchbull stood with hands on hips, glaring at him. "Get on with it!" she shouted. "Eat it up!"
Suddenly the boy let out a gigantic belch which rolled around the Assembly Hall like thunder. Many of the audience began to giggle.
"Silence!" shouted the Trunchbull.
The boy cut himself another thick slice and started eating it fast. There were still no signs of flagging or giving up. He certainly did not look as though he was about to stop and cry out, "I can't eat anymore! I'm going to be sick!" He was still in the running.

Roald Dahl, *Matilda*

I once watched an episode of *Oprah* about a woman who waited until her husband went to work each day, went to an all-you-can-eat restaurant by herself, gorged until she was about to burst, and then, out in her car, threw up everything into a bag that she hid in a wall of her house until trash day.

Until then, I thought no one could possibly be living the same life that I was.

I have been in many therapy sessions for bulimia, both one-on-one and in a group. In the group meetings, we were not allowed to talk about our methods as they might teach others something they didn't know, and they would then go home and try. Not only do we now live in the age of the internet where it is easy to find every method under the sun, but if you are truly in bondage to one of these kinds of addictions, the method is not what needs to be dealt with, it is the root cause. Until that is identified and sorted out, the behavior will only continue and worsen over time.

Before getting married, I could hide my disorder fairly easily. The bulimia was pretty severe before I was married, but the marriage escalated things in a few ways. I could no longer hide my behavior like I used to, nor did I have the money or freedom to go out whenever I wanted to get food to binge. Think having no money or freedom would take care of the bulimia? Think again. The second reason the disorder escalated is a crucial detail that addicts need to consider. What I was actually dealing with without knowing it was obsessive-compulsive disorder, which gets incredibly worse with trauma, hormonal change, and significant life changes in general. OCD will have a chapter all its own, but marrying my ex-husband was certainly a big, traumatic change to my life after tumultuous changes had already been happening since I was a kid.

Any addict to drugs and alcohol knows the overpowering "urge" to do the drug. If there is any way at all possible of doing the drug, it is getting done. The addict does not wake up in the morning wanting to ruin their lives. They do not want to disappoint everyone they love; they do not even want to do the drug! But they are in bondage to it and cannot escape. This is so difficult for those who do not have this kind of brain to comprehend. How on earth can someone constantly choose the drug over their loved ones—over their own children?

They are not. They do not love the substance more than their loved ones. They are held captive. But if you haven't experienced this, you cannot fathom this. No one wants to fathom it. If you cannot fathom this because you have never been in bondage to a chemical, thank God every day.

Does this explanation make it any easier on loved ones? No, not at all. Addiction is the worst for everyone involved. It is a wrecking ball to marriages, parenthood, and livelihood in every sense of the word. And it doesn't negate the fact that in order for the non-addict to thrive, they must remove themselves if the addict will not take the steps to get the help they need.

I am certain every addict feels their addiction is the most shameful, so of course, I felt my strange addiction to bingeing and purging was the most shameful. Drugs and alcohol are *acceptable* dependencies but eating your entire pantry and throwing it up five times a day is a complete sideshow. I still feel that way even though I know it isn't true. Every addiction is destruction, no matter what it is, and every addiction comes complete with a mountain of shame.

For five years, I was in the depths of despair. I could not stop, no matter how hard I tried. I would go to therapy. They would tell me that my upbringing was a factor and that I was in an unhealthy marriage, and I would get frustrated and quit. I didn't have time for all of that. What was I going to do now about my upbringing? And the husband saw no reason to change anything in the marriage. I saw no way out at the time, but I needed the behavior to stop immediately. I was literally killing myself! Every day, I would try again to not be an insane person, and every day I failed.

Trapped in every aspect of my life, bulimia became my life. Each day consisted of secretly planning, preparing, bingeing, purging, cleaning up, and replacing food before my husband got home. I had to sneak and steal food since I didn't have money of my own. One time, I was bingeing while driving and got pulled over for an illegal U-turn. The officer giving me the ticket had to think I was crazy. I was.

I was either working at Starbucks—sometimes bingeing and purging while at work—or in the bizarre plan-binge-purge-clean-replace cycle when I was alone at the house.

This went on day after day until one summer, we went to New Jersey for a week. Not only was I unable to binge and purge on the vacation, but the change of location and my husband's kind relatives made it so that I didn't feel the urge to. The day we got back from the trip, I started taking classes at a community college. This proved to be a fresh start for me, as I was able to get my footing a bit and live somewhat normally for a while. The bulimia wasn't gone, but I was able to stick to the structure of the classes, and I started exercising daily in the school's gym. I had gained weight since I was constantly bingeing and purging, and this new structure and exercise made that weight fall off. Things were looking up, and I was starting to look out—at a way out.

At this point, defeated by bulimia, sick of being trapped, hating the husband and his mother, and sick of being their roommate, any hint of Christianity that I had been holding on to, I threw to the birds. I was now a self-proclaimed atheist. Atheists had no reason not to get divorced. My mind was made up; I was getting in the best possible shape, I was getting divorced, and I was going back to dancing.

Chapter 10
The Time I was Almost a Millionaire

Wes breaks open the lucky nest and gives half to Magnus. He reads the fortune aloud, "Five, twenty-five, seventy-two, fifteen, eleven. Aw, come on! Lottery numbers? I'm not even old enough to play!"

Wes Prewitt, *Brumbletide and the Changing of the Crowns*

How about another funny story to break the tension? During my first marriage, I was always pondering ways to get out. One time, I planned on trying to win the lottery. I would have gotten in trouble if I had taken cash out of the bank account, but you know those tip jars at your coffee shop? Once a week, those are divided up amongst the baristas according to how many hours they have worked. Sometimes you would get ten dollars, but sometimes it was ninety! Of course, most of my tips went to bingeing and purging, but one time, I went into a gas station and bought a lottery ticket. I can't remember if it was

Mega Millions or Power Ball or what it was, but it wasn't a scratch-off. It was the kind where you had to pick the numbers and then see if you won on the news. The only time I was able to watch the news was in the morning when the husband was there, so I had to check online while he was at work.

The time had come. My heart beating fast, I pulled up the website. Could this actually be my way out? There was no way, right? When I found the day's drawing, I looked at each number carefully to make sure I got them right.

I got every winning number—but one.

I was *almost* a millionaire. Or maybe even a billionaire. But I had missed it by *one* number.

Disappointed, I thought to myself that perhaps maybe I still won some money, at least a few thousand. I checked again.

$175

I couldn't even buy anything nice because the husband would see it and wonder where I got the money to pay for it. I didn't want to binge away $175 even though I could. I ended up telling the husband I bought the ticket and missed millions by one number. I gave him the money.

So close, yet so far.

Chapter 11
Following the White Rabbit in Circles

Lewis Carroll, Alice's Adventures in Wonderland

Obsessive-compulsive disorder is the worst. Not only is this sneaky mental illness what was causing my mind to play tricks on me for so many years (aside from already suffering from the worst illness imaginable, spiritual blindness), but so many people are dealing with OCD and have no idea. In addition, not many people understand it, and because of this, they do not believe it is even a real problem at all. I share this story in the hope that my experience will lead those who have been suffering to get help. There is certainly help to be had. There is hope!

OCD is a mental and behavioral disorder where an individual experiences a severe fear response to common thoughts, often due to an overactive molecular signal pathway in the amygdala. The fear response causes the thought to become an obsession. These are called intrusive thoughts because the dooming thoughts keep coming back even though they are unwanted. The individual then engages in compulsions that temporarily relieve the anxiety.

Further explanation would be if two people are waiting on a train; one has OCD, the other does not. Both people are likely to have the strange thought of *what if I jumped in front of the train?*

The person without OCD has the thought, boards the train, and moves on with their day. But the person with OCD experiences an intense fear response to the thought, not at all by choice, giving them the feeling that they need to protect themselves from actually jumping in front of the train. They will then knowingly or unknowingly begin engaging in compulsions. They may take a certain number of steps to the train each time they board. They may only sit in a certain seat—a seat with a certain number. They may say certain prayers or mantras before boarding or during the ride.

The compulsions do, in fact, relieve the anxiety for a short time, but the individual must keep engaging in the compulsions in order to keep feeling relief. But the more one acts out the compulsions, the worse and worse the anxiety surrounding the obsession becomes, and it all ends up a perpetual and worsening mess of anxiety and eventually insanity.

As stated in the last chapter, OCD is always there in a person. Some have this kind of brain; some do not. It is common in families where addiction is prevalent. A person may live many years without a problem and then wonder why they seemingly spontaneously go crazy after a marriage, baby, or divorce. This is because "flare-ups" happen in response to trauma, hormonal change, and significant life changes in general, good or bad. Many people have been slugging through this for years with no clue and are soaked in shame because they cannot seem to roll with life's punches like everyone else.

Both the OCD brain and non-OCD brain have a responsibility to their family, work, and community. Having OCD does not excuse that. But if you are educated on the disorder and receive the proper tools as early as possible, you will not keep failing in your responsibilities as you may have until now.

During my childhood, my obsessions centered around the end of the world, and my compulsions were prayers and mantras. I have always fixated on numbers which is funny considering I am so bad at math! I would only get out of bed at times that added up to be seven, do absolutely nothing on a six, and would assign significance to certain days of the month according to their number.

It isn't always, but my bulimia was an OCD compulsion, and the behavior worsened with each hormonal change and trauma. Trauma comes in all shapes and sizes, and every one of them affects the OCD brain.

The shame was so heavy at times, on top of exhaustion from throwing up all the time, that I often couldn't get out of bed. I missed work and events, continually disappointing my co-workers, family, and myself. I couldn't get it together.

It is so easy to say, "Well, you just gotta...." I understand this. Not being mentally ill these past seven years, this phrase runs through my mind when someone is perpetually struggling. It's funny how we forget the pain of traumatic things. We do not forget that it was traumatic, but we forget the magnitude of pain we felt at the time. If we felt the pain of childbirth all the time, the population would be much less. But we forget the pain and do it all over again. This is a blessing. It is so easy for someone who does not have crippling feelings of fear and overpowering binge urges to say, "You just gotta stop." "You just gotta get it together." and the most shame-inducing, "I had no choice to be mentally ill. I had to *fill in the blank with work, raise children, etc.*" as if it was a choice. It is a choice whether to get help for mental illness or not, but mental illness is not a choice, just as catching a cold is not a choice.

Another misconception is that mental illness is something recent. Mental illness has always been around. Chronic anxiety, depression, and addiction have ruined lives for millennia.

Saying, "You just gotta..." is the equivalent of telling someone who has broken their leg, "That doesn't hurt that bad.

You are fine. Get up and walk." At the same time, the person saying this walks on two healthy legs. If you haven't experienced living with addiction or anxiety disorders, you cannot imagine what it is like or how one would deal with it, and the seemingly logical explanation is that the person is a degenerate who doesn't want to succeed in life. They do not love their family. They do not care for their friends. They cannot keep a job because they simply do not want to. The proof is that, "Well, I can."

Break your leg, think the pain away, and go about your daily tasks. Then you will be in the place where you can tell others with broken legs to get up and walk.

I fell face-first through life in this miserable way until I became a mother. Becoming a mother brings with it massive hormonal and life changes. It was after having kids that my obsessions shifted from my body to another body—that of my son Ryan.

Chapter 12

Rumpelstiltskin

As soon as the girl was left alone, the little man appeared for the third time and said: "What will you give me if I spin the straw for you this time?"

"I have nothing left to give," answered the girl. "Then you must promise me the first child you have after you are queen," said the little man. "But who knows whether that will happen?" thought the girl; but as she did not know what else to do in her necessity, she promised the little man what he desired, upon which he began to spin until all the straw was gold. And when in the morning the king came and found all done according to his wish, he caused the wedding to be held at once, and the miller's pretty daughter became a queen.

In a year's time she brought a fine child into the world and thought no more of the little man; but one day he came suddenly into her room and said: "Now give me what you promised me."

The queen was terrified greatly and offered the little man all the riches of the kingdom if he would only leave the child.

But the little man said: "No, I would rather have something living than all the treasures of the world." Then the queen began to lament and to weep, so that the little man had pity upon her. "I will give you three days," said he, "and if at the end of that time you cannot tell my name, you must give up the child to me."

The Brothers Grimm, *Rumpelstiltskin*

Not every bulimic who has OCD is a narcissist, but I certainly was. Every minute of every day was spent thinking of the comfort and well-being of one individual—me. I am still pretty self-absorbed, but the fact that I am at least aware of it and try not to be is a miracle in itself.

I got pregnant on purpose in 2012 and had second thoughts the whole time. I did not feel like I knew the baby in my belly that was completely wreaking havoc on the inside and outside of my body. Blindsided by morning sickness, healthy food repulsed me. I had planned to be a "fit mom" but could hardly stand to even look at anything fibrous. White crackers and even pizza were more tolerable than grilled chicken and broccoli. I gained the most weight in my first trimester and, yes, threw up several times on purpose. I felt much better in the second and third trimesters but worried constantly about how I would get enough sleep (sleep is important for weight loss) and fit in my workouts once the baby arrived.

I wrote out a sleeping and eating schedule that I expected the baby and me to follow. My friend, Emily, laughed when I told her about it because she knew a baby does not care about any schedule.

Ryan Jacob Teal was born on November 1st, 2012. He was a squeamish little night owl, and I was madly in love with him. I loved watching him sleep and eat and cry and smile—I loved all of it! I had come to believe in God again before this but experiencing the love a mother has for her baby, there was no doubt in my mind now that there was a God, and it was quite possible that He loved us like *this*. The miraculous bond between mother and child had to be from the hand of a good Creator.

But as much as my heart soared, my mind reeled. Though I was still bulimic, my obsession was no longer with my body and weight; I was obsessed with Ryan. What if something terrible happened to him? How would I be able to go on? I wouldn't. Every time I looked at the sweet little baby in my midst, I was equally filled with awe, joy, and immense sadness.

Still unaware of OCD and that I was experiencing it, I became incredibly disturbed by the constant intrusive thoughts. I prayed and prayed for God to protect Ryan and would even ask God in prayer to tell me if Ryan was going to die, hoping the answer that came into my mind would be "No."

I had so much to learn back then about God and how He speaks and OCD and how it speaks. God speaks, but not on demand, and very rarely audibly or in words that pop into your mind. God speaks through His word, the Bible. He speaks through providence. He speaks through suffering. And God was certainly speaking to me through my suffering, though I did not know it at the time.

When I knelt down and asked God if Ryan would die in my lifetime and heard in my mind a "Yes," God *was* speaking to me, but not in the way I thought at the moment. The thing that said "Yes" was the OCD. God was telling me through my anguish to read His Bible, which I had never read in my life. He was speaking to me then, and He was about to speak to me *loudly*. I just needed to open the Book first.

I white-knuckled postpartum anxiety and depression unknowingly until I got pregnant with my daughter in 2016. It was this hormonal and life change that would do me in. It wouldn't be long after the birth of Anna that I would go off the rails mentally to the point that my life would come to a screeching halt.

It was good that I was afflicted...this was all happening by none other than God Himself. I was in pain, I was in anguish, I wanted it to stop the whole time it was happening. When we are suffering, we are paying so much attention to the pain that we have no idea that it may just be the best thing that ever happened to us. In turmoil, it is almost impossible to look at your life as a whole and deduce that it has not been going in a good way, and perhaps this is God changing everything for the better.

"You're exactly where you need to be," my mother said kindly but confidently after I sobbed to her everything that was going on.

I didn't believe her, but she was right. This terror and pain was the beginning of God rescuing me from the bondage I'd been in for decades.

Chapter 13
Thestrals

"Can't...can't you see them?"

"See what?"

"Can't you see what's pulling the carriages?"

Ron looked seriously alarmed now.

"Are you feeling all right, Harry?"

"I...yeah..."

Harry felt utterly bewildered. The horse was there in front of him, gleaming solidly in the dim light issuing from the station windows behind them, vapor rising from its nostrils in the chilly night air. Yet unless Ron was faking—and it was a very feeble joke if he was—Ron could not see it at all.

"Shall we get in then?" said Ron uncertainly, looking at Harry as though worried about him.

"Yeah," said Harry. "Yeah, go on..."

"It's all right," said a dreamy voice from behind Harry as Ron vanished into the coach's dark interior. "You're not going mad or anything. I can see them too."

"Can you?" said Harry desperately, turning to Luna. He could see the bat-winged horses reflected in her wide, silvery eyes.

"Oh yes," said Luna, "I've been able to see them ever since my first day here. They've always pulled the carriages. Don't worry. You're just as sane as I am."

J.K. Rowling, *Harry Potter and the Order of the Phoenix*

etting pregnant with my daughter was the straw that broke the mentally ill camel's back. I went from crazy to insane (although, apparently, you are not truly insane until you do not know you are insane.) Not only was I incredibly depressed for the duration of the pregnancy, but I was convinced that having a baby girl instead of another boy was going to ruin our lives. Many women try everything possible to have a baby, experiencing the pain of miscarriage along the way. They would kill for a baby boy *or* girl, and here I was, furious that I wasn't getting another boy. All I can say is that I had lost my mind. So ridiculous.

The minute Anna was born, and I heard that precious little girl cry, I loved her. They handed me the beautiful bundle that looked me straight in my eyes with her big, sweet, blue ones. I loved her to infinity and back again and felt like the biggest idiot for thinking I didn't want a girl.

But the depressed and delusional pregnancy was only the beginning. Postpartum anxiety reared its ugly head, and this time with fangs. The OCD was in overdrive, and my obsession that Ryan was going to die was worse than ever.

The thing about these anxiety disorders is that the episodes are always just different enough that you can't for sure chalk it up to anxiety. A new panic attack is never exactly the same as the one before it, leaving you wondering if it really is a heart attack or stroke this time. And then, of course, there is the neverending untied loose end that your fear could quite possibly come true. Terrible things happen to people all the time!

If this intrusive fear was some sort of postpartum anxiety, why didn't my fears revolve around my *current* baby? Instead, I was still stuck on the first one, even though I loved both of them equally.

By this time, I had Googled backward and forward every symptom I experienced, so postpartum depression and anxiety were on my radar, but OCD was not. The logical explanation for this overwhelming, never-ending "gut feeling" was that I was having premonitions of my son's death in order to prepare me for it. I'd heard my whole life to listen to my gut, and it seemed to be screaming at the moment. Tragedy might be inevitable, but I could try to keep it from happening or at least prepare myself mentally.

When you are constantly terrified something is going to happen, your brain, trying to help you survive the perceived doom, begins finding proof that your fear is valid. Like Thestrals, what you are seeing is actually there, but no one else sees it like you do. Your brain picks out specific things to show you proof of your fear. Everything I watched on television, everything I saw on the internet, every conversation, *everything* showed a sign that my worst fear was going to come true. Every single hour of every single day, my brain was alerting me to the fact that Ryan's death was imminent, and no matter what I did, I couldn't get away from the constant thoughts and visions.

My brain was eating me alive.

The anxiety got so bad that it became very physical. Almost all day long, I had dizziness, tremors, shortness of breath, numbness in my extremities and face, blurry vision—so many symptoms! They would always erupt into a panic attack at some point, which sometimes would result in a call to the paramedics. It feels like you are dying. It is so real while it is happening. I couldn't drive long distances and had to take breaks while showering to keep from falling over.

I was never suicidal. God was one of my greatest fears at the time, after all. The last thing I wanted to do was face Him before I absolutely had to. But I know why people do commit suicide. They get sick and tired of fighting their own brain all day, every day. They are exhausted—past exhausted. They are not living. There seems to be no light at the end of the tunnel. No end to the tunnel at all.

But little did I know God was using all of this to show me who He was and what He did for me—and you!

Light was about to peek in.

But first, a story!

Chapter 14
The Star of Bethlehem

Now after Jesus was born in Bethlehem of Judea in the days of Herod the king,
behold, wise men from the east came to Jerusalem, saying, "Where is he who
has been born king of the Jews? For we saw his star when it rose and have
come to worship him." When Herod the king heard this, he was troubled, and
all Jerusalem with him; and assembling all the chief priests and scribes of the
people, he inquired of them where the Christ was to be born. They told him, "In
Bethlehem of Judea: for so it is written by the prophet:

"'And you, O Bethlehem, in the land of Judah,

are by no means least among the rulers of Judah;

for from you shall come a ruler,

who will shepherd my people Israel.'"

Then Herod summoned the wise men secretly and ascertained from them what
time the star appeared. And he sent them to Bethlehem, saying, "Go and search
diligently for the child, and when you have found him, bring me word, that I
too may come and worship him. After listening to the king, they went on their
way. And behold, the star that they had seen when it rose went before them
until it came to rest over the place where the child was. When they saw the star,
they rejoiced exceedingly with great joy. And going into the house, they saw
the child with Mary his mother, and they fell down and worshipped him. Then,
opening their treasures, they offered him gifts, gold and frankincense and

myrrh. And being warned in a dream not to return to Herod, they departed to their own country by another way.

Matthew 2:1-10

This story is significant because it shows that all the demons from my childhood were still happily at home in my brain diligently fanning the flames of the fire of insanity. Remember the story about *The Omen* and the end of the world? Even after two decades full of rebellion and even becoming an atheist at one point, at thirty-one, I was still afraid of the end of the world.

Call to me and I will answer you,
and will tell you great and hidden things
that you have not known.
Jeremiah 33:3

When you are terrified, and you call out to God, He will answer you one day. And it may just be when you least expect it. This fear of the end of the world was planted in me when I was a kid, and I believed. Then life happened, and I became less and less fearful. I was living my usual self-absorbed life when Jason and I were sitting together on a June summer night. Jason was scrolling his phone, and casually mentioned, "Oh look, the Star of Bethlehem is coming."

I lost my breath and dropped everything to see what he was talking about. He showed me the video. Sure enough, Jeff Hill, the Fox 5 weatherman, was saying a Venus/Jupiter conjunction would appear in the sky on June 30th for a rare "Star of Bethlehem" moment that had not happened in two thousand years. Our wedding anniversary is June 30th. In my mind, the fact that the Star of Bethlehem would appear on our wedding anniversary made it more significant and even more likely that this was a sign of the end. Do you see how the OCD does? For things that are not significant, your brain finds tiny connections, little "proofs," and yells, "Pay attention! Pay attention!" This is wonderful for fantasy novel writing. This is not at all wonderful for living life in general.

Regardless, Romans 8:28 rings true. Everything works together for the good of those who love God. I had never read the Bible at this point, only parts of it, but I had been obsessed with the end of the world for decades, and the Star of Bethlehem shining again for the first time in two thousand years certainly seemed like an end-time event. Mind you, I had never read the book of Revelation because it was too terrifying to face. Mom had read some of it to me, but I was eight.

Now after Jesus was born in Bethlehem of Judea in the days of Herod the king, behold, wise men from the east came to Jerusalem, saying, "Where is he who has been born king of the Jews? For we saw his star when it rose and have come to worship him."

The star had risen when Jesus was born. The star shining again had to mean that Jesus was certainly returning, and there I was, caught with my narcissistic pants down.

I shaped up and quick. I went back to church and tried my very best to be the most Christian I could possibly be. I made food for my friends and gave away my things. I did anything and everything I could think of to "be good" because everywhere I looked, there were signs of the end. Even the clouds looked like God was in them. I had to be good. But reading the Bible was still something too difficult to do.

On September 7th of that year, I felt a pulling to read the book of Revelation. Jason had taken Ryan to his mother's for the day; Anna hadn't been born yet. I ignored the pull for a while and then finally gave in. If the world was going down in flames soon, why not read about it beforehand? I was already reeling in terror; how much worse could it make things?

Reading the book of Revelation was one of the most amazing experiences I had ever had up until then. I read every page of Revelation in perfect peace. It was like God was telling me, "It's alright. There isn't anything to be afraid of."

I hung on every word, and to my surprise, half of the things I had thought were in Revelation all those years were not! I thought, if what I had been told was in Revelation wasn't really in there, what about the rest of the Bible? I needed to read it all. So, I waited another few years to start because why do today what you can put off until tomorrow?

Thinking back, it is somewhat challenging to pinpoint when I was actually converted to a true Christian. Was I saved when I prayed, "Now I lay me down to sleep" when I was little? Was it when I watched *The Omen*? Or was it when I was baptized at ten? Perhaps it was at twenty-five when I was baptized for the second time and then became an atheist. Was it when I saw the

Star of Bethlehem? Or was it after the events I have not mentioned yet? I will leave it up to you to decide, but it has been said that faith alone saves, but faith that saves is never alone. In my heart, I know I have only been truly awake and alive for seven years.

I did eventually come to know Jesus—and that is salvation—and He did do exactly what He said He would.

Behold, I stand at the door and knock. If anyone hears my voice and opens the door, I will come in to him and eat with him, and he with me.

Revelation 3:20

Chapter 15
The Dragon

He had turned into a dragon while he was asleep. Sleeping on a dragon's hoard with dragonish thoughts in his heart, he had become a dragon himself.

That explained everything. There had been no two dragons beside him in the cave. The claws to the right and left had been his own right and left claws. The two columns of smoke had been coming from his own nostrils. As for the pain in his left arm (or what had been his left arm) he could now see what had happened by squinting with his left eye. The bracelet which had been fitted very nicely on the upper arm of a boy was far too small for the thick, stumpy foreleg of a dragon.

C.S. Lewis, The Voyage of the Dawn Treader

How in the world, after attending church since nine years old, being baptized twice, and being so terrified of the apocalypse that I started going church again in my thirties and bending over backward to "be good," could I still think I didn't know God until 2017? The answer is that even after returning to church and trying to act my best, I still did not know the Gospel. I did not know the Gospel of Jesus Christ, I did not have that truth planted in good soil in my heart, and because of this one thing I had missed, this one *crucial* thing, I was not a New Creation. You can be a follower of Jesus and not be saved. You must be born again, and I wasn't. Like poor Eustace, I was still asleep on a dragon hoard, thinking dragonish thoughts, and even after being scared out of my wits thinking it was the end of the world, I was still a dragon myself.

The Bible says that unless Jesus is our "Vine" and we are his "branches," we can do nothing of any worth. Connected to the Vine, we have all the nourishment we need to bear beautiful fruit that will then nourish others. Trying to act like the best Christian I could after being scared out of my wits was as if I was sticking plastic fruit on a vine, hoping for the same result. The fruit isn't really connected and will fall off easily. Not to mention, plastic fruit doesn't nourish anyone and may even cause harm if ingested.

I was not connected to the Vine, and, therefore, was not bearing any real spiritual fruit for myself or anyone else. Thankfully, the story doesn't end there, but little did I know then that just ahead, the valley would get much deeper and much darker, and the true Jesus Himself would be waiting for me in the midst of it.

As I am writing this, it is right at seven years since the dream that changed everything. As stated, I was already losing it when I gave birth to Anna, and afterward, I was in constant dread that something terrible was going to happen any minute. But my fear was about to get exponentially worse.

It was the night of May 7th, 2017. I fell asleep for just ten minutes or so and had the most strange and vivid dream.

I was in our basement watching Ryan dance around plumes of smoke when a gleaming, multicolored snake suddenly slithered out from the corner, grew to be giant, and swallowed Ryan whole! The snake then unswallowed him, and the next thing I knew Ryan was behind me, all dressed in white.

I said to him, "Are you okay?"

"Yes," he said, "And look at me! I have a new body!"

And when I woke up, I was haunted that God was telling me through the dream that Ryan was going to die and go to heaven.

Reading the dream, you might get no notion that the dream meant that Ryan would die. But to my OCD brain obsessed with the intrusive thought, this was the nail in Ryan's coffin. He was going to die, and God was letting me know that he would go to heaven, where he would be dressed in white with a new body.

I was distraught.

I didn't eat. I prayed and prayed that God wouldn't take Ryan in my lifetime. The intrusive thoughts were constant, the physical symptoms out of control. I couldn't even get through a shower or a drive without having to stop because of the dizziness. All the time, I had that heart-pounding, fight-or-flight airiness you get when you think someone has broken into your house in the middle of the night. I was dizzy when I stood up. I was dizzy when I sat down. I would lie down, and the room would spin in circles around me.

I had lost it. I was sad and depressed and petrified out of my mind. To the outsider looking in, nothing was wrong. I had a happy marriage, two beautiful and healthy children—nothing was wrong. But on the inside, everything was burning to the ground.

But it was none other than God, in His great mercy and grace, who had started the fire.

Though I saw no way forward, alone in the pitch-black tunnel, afraid to take a step, He made a way where there was no way. I couldn't fathom it then, but God was about to grow a glorious garden out of dust and ashes.

A week from the dream was Mother's Day, and the church we were attending was having a baby dedication ceremony that I had already planned to bring Anna to. But after a week of agonizing over the dream, I walked up to the front of the church with *both* kids, even though Ryan had already been dedicated when he was a baby.

We were supposed to choose a Bible verse to be read during their dedication. I opened the Bible straight to Acts 1:8.

But you will receive power when the Holy Spirit has come upon you, and you will be my witnesses in Jerusalem and in all Judea and Samaria, and to the end of the earth.

I opened the Bible and chose the first verse I saw because that is how I did it back then. I followed my feelings, thinking they were God, and took a "fortune cookie" approach to the Bible, taking verses out of context to fit them to what I wanted them to mean. This was not a relationship with the God of the Bible because I did not care to pay attention to what exactly He was trying to express through His word. Even though I was afraid, I still hadn't submitted to the fact that God was a real being with a better plan than mine. I had not given my life to God. I was still holding on with white knuckles to what I thought I wanted. I was still making my own plans and asking God to bless those. Still, even afraid and hoping God didn't bring doom to my life, I was only in a relationship with myself.

I had been in church since I was nine years old when my mother became a Christian and started taking us. Just like in school, I only paid attention to the few things that interested me. I was now thirty-four years old and had called myself a Christian for decades, except for when I ditched it altogether that one time. I had never read the Bible, not even when I was scared to death by the Star of Bethlehem. I didn't intend to read it, either. I liked listening to sermons and reading devotionals sometimes, but the Bible was too difficult.

But God would radically save me through the reading of the Bible. For a while after this happened, I said that a person cannot be genuinely saved without having read the Bible. Now I know this is not true. While I do believe it is crucial for a person claiming to be a Christian to study the Bible thoroughly, a person is saved when they truly understand the Gospel of Jesus Christ and it so happened that God used the Bible to pierce my heart with that truth. I now know that God can pierce someone's heart with the Gospel however He wants. But the fact remains that to be saved and to be transformed into the unmistakable New Creation in Christ, one must understand the depth of what Christ did for them on the cross. And the Bible, the whole thing read in context, drives the truth of what Christ Jesus did for us into the heart like a hot knife through butter.

Until May 7th, 2017, I believed that Jesus was real. I even believed He died on the cross for my sins like you believe when someone tells you they went to work that day. But I didn't understand what that meant. It was as if your father had told you he went to work that day. You believed him. What reason did you have not to? But what you didn't realize was that during work that day, he went to court, where a criminal was sentenced to life in prison for a crime. Your completely innocent father, who himself was a husband, father, and beloved teacher, stood up in the court and, willing to walk away from all that he loves, said, "I'll go to prison instead of them. Let them go free."

The rest of the story changes everything! And the rest of the story of "Christ died on the cross and rose again" changed everything. All those years, I had missed the whole point.

The dream about Ryan ended up doing many things that would change life as I knew it forever. The first thing is that it drove me into finally reading the Bible I had planned on never reading even though I superficially said I would. No more verses of the day acting as little fortunes. No more Philippians 4:13 telling me I could run five miles to nowhere to be skinny through Christ who strengthens me. No more Jeremiah 29:11 telling me that God knows the plans He has for me—His plans seemed pretty bleak at the moment. No more asking for anything in Christ's name so He would do it without fully knowing Christ first.

God had terrified me with a dream. Or had He? Did God speak through dreams? I watched every sermon imaginable and could not get a straight answer. Now I know that even if there had been a straight answer to this on the internet, God would not have let me find it. Because with no other choice, out of sheer desperation, I opened the Bible and read straight through the whole thing from Genesis to Revelation searching for the answer I wanted to be *no*.

This single act opened the door for God to speak to me for real. My feelings were not speaking to me this time. This was not my obsessive thoughts shouting fears and propelling me into compulsions. This was much different. It was indeed the LORD of the universe, sitting with me, talking with me, telling me His story. The book of Hebrews says the word of God is alive and active. I testify this is certainly true. Of course, after telling you how insane I was, you must read it for yourself because I cannot be trusted.

Through the Old Testament stories, God opened my eyes to His holiness and my sin—and how my sin rendered me unable to be in the presence of His Holiness. Not only that, but a holy

God, a God who is wholly righteous, cannot dwell with sin. Of course He can't. For us to be with God in any way, sin cannot be present. My sin had canceled me out. And since God loves His creation and wants to be with His creation, sin has to go. *I had to go.*

For the wages of sin is death...

My eyes were opened. I was soaked in sin. I had done terrible things my whole life. I had caused a mountain of harm that I was too self-absorbed to see. And the wrong things I had been doing thinking they were not all that bad because, well, everyone did them, were canceling me out in the eyes of God. And if that were not enough, the sins I spent my life trying to stop were canceling me out too. I was still a bulimic! This sin was completely out of my control. God cannot possibly cancel me out for that too.

He cannot dwell with sin.

It was becoming glaringly apparent that while I had grown up in a society that touted how we all deserve the best things in life, in the eyes of God, I not only deserved punishment but death, and if it was dependent on how I had been living up until then, I did not deserve for Ryan to live. If I was to receive my payback, if justice was to be served, I deserved punishment. And the worst punishment was to lose a child.

By the time I got through the book about Job, who was a righteous man whom God allowed so much tragedy to happen, it was clear that an unrighteous woman like me was doomed.

Opening the Bible for the answer to my problem had made things exponentially worse. You know the story in Daniel where King Nebuchadnezzar was cast off to dwell among wild animals because of his pride, and he began eating grass and living in insanity? I feel like I wasn't too far from that at this point in time.

There was no choice now. Paralyzed with fear and crippled with constant physical anxiety symptoms, I had to get help for my mental illness. Therapy is also one of the many things the dream caused to happen. I scanned the names on the insurance list. Sarah Beth Wheeler wasn't far from my house. No, too country.

I chose another name from the list in a bigger city. I saw her for a few months until she told me my dream would probably come true. Back to the list. Back to the name Sarah Beth Wheeler.

I left a message, and she called back. She had a soft, kind voice. She sounded young. I would go one time. It would be nice to get out of my head for an hour, but she was certainly not going to be the one to help me.

Chapter 16
Winter

Nine months I saw Sarah Beth. God had used a strange dream to simultaneously get me to read His Bible, treat the OCD, and, best of all, give me His glorious life-giving Gospel.

I walked into the old, brick, uninviting building that was Barrow Ministry Village. A tree fell on it that year. It looked like the kind of building a tree would fall on. But it was surprisingly pretty inside. Sarah Beth was behind the desk. She had a kind face and warm disposition. She signed me in herself, and she seemed like she was really happy to see me. Whether doctors are actually happy to see me or not, I like when they at least act like it. She called me back to her office. I sat down and proceeded to sob out everything that had happened and was happening.

All of it.

I was so sick of it all. I was sick of being sick. Sick of being scared. Sick of thinking. Sick of feeling. Sick of crying. Sick of humiliation and shame. Sick of not being able to stop. I had nothing to lose in telling her all of the insane things that I had been thinking and doing.

I laid it all out to Sarah Beth in case she might be able to help me. I told her about watching *The Omen* as a kid and being afraid of the end of the world. I told her about Bully Riggins at the lunch table. I told her about dropping out of school and leaving home. I told her all the strange things about the bulimia and the depths of despair. I told her about Waffle House and Hooters and Pink Pony. I told her about the awful relationships and the awful marriage and about getting married again immediately after getting divorced. I told her about my kids and that I was obsessed with the notion that one of them would die soon.

I remember telling her about my obsession with Ryan. I was already sobbing, but whatever was worse than sobbing, I did that. I told her that if God was going to take Ryan, I understood that He had a plan that I didn't see, but I couldn't seem to get away from the sadness of it.

Sarah Beth sat there listening and finally said, "You are mourning your son who hasn't died."

And she was right. I was living in perpetual sadness and doom of a future that may never come. It was killing me.

Sarah Beth went on to teach me about the nature of obsessive-compulsive disorder and how to take my thoughts captive. Her help, along with medication, is what God used to finally free me from the bondage of bulimia and OCD. After decades of trying and failing to kick the bulimia, I had given in to the idea that it was always going to be the dark side of me that I would have to fight against until I died. It is this that is why I sympathize with addicts and homosexuals. When something has a hold of you like that, even something you hate, you cannot simply quit alone. But as written earlier, even when we cannot stop, we have a responsibility to try to stop and to keep trying, even if we have to try our whole lives.

The timeline of events leading up to and during treatment with Sarah Beth is important because it shows God's timing and that all of this happened by His hand alone. First, I had Anna on September 12th, 2016, and began experiencing severe postpartum anxiety and depression symptoms. On May 7th, 2017, I had the dream of Ryan and the snake that sent me spiraling into obsessive-compulsive oblivion. Desperate to learn whether God still speaks to us in dreams, I finally opened the Bible and began reading from cover to cover. Through the Old Testament, God opened my eyes to who He is and the sin that was keeping me apart from Him. Feeling much worse and riddled with physical anxiety symptoms, I went to Sarah Beth and began medication in

October of 2017. The physical symptoms decreased dramatically, and I was able to focus on therapy.

The bulimia went away.

After twenty years of bondage and suffering, the bulimia was gone. I couldn't believe it.

I continued seeing Sarah Beth for nine months, all the while continuing to read through the Bible. By the time I got to the New Testament, I had a total belief in God like never before. Still, I was terrified that He would strike me—or worse, Ryan—dead at any second to justifiably pay me back for my multitude of wrongdoings. It wouldn't make any sense for Him not to.

So when I opened the New Testament, I was extremely interested in what exactly Jesus paid for with His death on the cross. He couldn't possibly have taken care of *all* the punishment I deserved. That wouldn't be justice.

And this is when I was told the absolutely scandalous "good news" that I'd heard about many times but never paid attention to.

I asked Sarah Beth one day, "What did Jesus actually die for? So that we can go to heaven, right? I still have to pay here on earth for all the things I've done. He didn't pay for all of that too."

"He did! That's the Gospel!" Sarah Beth exclaimed, throwing up her hand.

"*That's* the Gospel?" I replied in disbelief.

And there it was, the Gospel. Justice had actually not been served in the way it should have, and instead, the Grace of all graces had been given through Jesus's death on the cross. Sure, if I robbed a bank, I would have to go to jail. If I cheated on my spouse, I would probably end up with another divorce. But as far as God inflicting death on me because of my sins, shockingly, Christ has taken that punishment on Himself. God had used all of my failures, mistakes, and worries to lead me to true life in His powerful, transforming Gospel of Jesus Christ. And if that wasn't enough, the next stop was Luke 7 in my journey through the Bible.

A woman in that town who lived a sinful life learned that Jesus was eating at the Pharisee's house, so she came there with an alabaster jar of perfume.

Luke 7:37

A woman who lived a sinful life—that was me.

As she stood behind him at his feet weeping, she began to wet his feet with her tears. Then she wiped them with her hair, kissed them and poured perfume on them.

When the Pharisee who had invited him saw this, he said to himself, "If this man were a prophet, he would know who is touching him and what kind of woman she is—that she is a sinner."

And Jesus answering said to him, "Simon, I have something to say to you."

And he answered, "Say it, Teacher."

A certain money lender had two debtors. One owed five hundred denarii, and the other fifty. When they could not pay, he canceled the debt of both. Now which of them will love him more?"

Simon answered, "The one, I suppose, for whom he cancelled the larger debt."

And he said to him, "You have judged rightly." Then turning toward the woman he said to Simon, "Do you see this woman? I entered your house; you gave me no water for my feet, but she has wet my feet with her tears and wiped them with her hair. You gave me no kiss, but from the time I came in she has not ceased to kiss my feet. You did not anoint my head with oil, but she has anointed my feet with ointment. Therefore I tell you, her sins, which are many, are forgiven—for she loved much. But he who is forgiven little, loves little." And he said to her, "Your sins are forgiven." Then those who were at the table with him began to say among themselves, "Who is this, who even forgives sins?" And he said to the woman, "Your faith has saved you; go in peace."

Luke 7:38-50

Go in peace! I told Sarah Beth what I had read, and she said, "Go in peace—it's like a command!"

I cried tears of joy that morning in Luke 7 at God's incredible mercy and grace that He has poured out on us in Jesus. I had been living in constant terror that God was going to take away my son to pay me back what I deserve, while the truth is that He punished His own Son instead of punishing me.

Jesus had, in fact, taken the punishment I deserve. Justice was not served. A flood of grace had been given. For unto us a Child was born.

Soli Deo Gloria. Glory to God alone.

Chapter 17
Unswallowed

I expect you've seen someone put a lighted match to a bit of newspaper which is propped up in a grate against an unlit fire. And for a second nothing seems to have happened; and then you notice a tiny streak of flame creeping along the edge of the newspaper. It was like that now. For a second after Aslan breathed on him the stone lion looked the same. Then a tiny streak of gold began to run along his white marble back—then it spread—then the color seemed to lick all over him as the flame licks all over a bit of paper—then, while his hindquarters were still obviously stone, the lion shook his mane and all the heavy, stone folds rippled into living hair. Then he opened a great red mouth, warm and living, and gave a prodigious yawn. And now his hindlegs had come to life. He lifted one of them and scratched himself. Then having caught sight of Aslan, he went bounding after him and frisking around him whimpering with delight and jumping to lick his face.

C.S. Lewis, *The Lion the Witch and the Wardrobe*

Since I was a kid, I heard about believers in Jesus being "New Creations." I believed it until I didn't, but I never was one until I actually was. When Sarah Beth told me the Gospel that day, it was finally planted in good soil in my heart, and I began to be *changed.* It has almost been seven years to the day since this adventure began, and I am still wholly changed.

It is talked about that when Jesus saves us, we then have heaven to look forward to, but it is less talked about how wonderful life on earth is after becoming a Christian. I think it is much more noticeable for those of us who have made abysmal decisions in the past. Whoever has been forgiven much loves much!

Christ doing away with my "old self" and bringing forth a New Creation is not just good for me, which it is very good for me, but it is also better for everyone in my life, in my nation, and in the world, because Jesus has, here on earth, changed my thoughts, feelings, and desires (without any help from me) for the better and He will only continue. I am convinced the more of these New Creations in Jesus that are made, the better the world will be. The Gospel of Jesus Christ will save the world.

When God opens your eyes to your sin and then how Jesus paid for it with His death on the cross, we are miraculously changed. We slowly become "unswallowed" by death. Our natural self, born in sin, begins dying, and our New Self begins springing forth without any effort on our part. I want to tell you this because it is real, and if you have or have not called yourself a Christian up until this moment, ask God to open your eyes to the truth about who you are and who He is. I urge you to do this whether you already believe in God or not. What harm will it do? As

Madeleine L'Engle says in *Many Waters, "Some things have to be believed to be seen."*

Do not be afraid to call out to God and ask this even if you have called yourself a Christian for many years. If you do not feel that you are this New Creation, call out to God! There is no time like the present, and you are definitely not alone. I thought I was a Christian for decades without really being one, and I know I am not a one-off case.

As someone who was the worst, I am here to testify that I am different today than I was before without trying. After the Star of Bethlehem, I tried to be good but wasn't really. When God changes you, it is unmistakable and genuine. Yes, I still sin. I still get mad, sad, and jealous. I still mess things up royally. But my thoughts, feelings, and actions are much more congruent with the Fruit of the Spirit in Galatians than I could have ever tried to make them be on my own. Things I didn't even realize could change, He changed.

An example of this is that I never imagined being happy for other people's success. I hated to see people succeed while I continued to waste away in the bed I made for myself. But I am genuinely happy for other's success now, and this is God's doing. I would have never thought of trying to change that about myself. How can you change feelings? Feelings just happen to you. But here I am, different.

ESTRANGING NOVEM

But the fruit of the Spirit is love, joy, peace, forbearance, kindness, goodness, faithfulness, gentleness and self-control. Against such things there is no law.

Galatians 5:22-23

We need Jesus to kill our natural selves with His death on the cross and resurrect us with Him into New Life—true life. We can try all day long to be better and to do good in the world, and we can even succeed, but true life and true righteousness, the kind that is felt on the inside and outside and all the way through, are found in Jesus. You may be skeptical, but again, what would it hurt to call out to God and see?

Jesus paid the punishment that I deserve with His own life. He was tortured, humiliated, and put to death—all of the things we want to happen to those who commit the most abominable crimes. Jesus, who never committed one crime, died instead of criminals like me so that we could live and experience the miraculous transformation that His resurrection gives. Jesus died and came back to life so the most unlikely characters could become the light of the world.

The dream I was so terrified would come true was, in fact, from God, but not in the way that I thought. It stopped me in my tracks, got me to be still and read the Bible that I had neglected for far too long, drove me to get the help I desperately needed that finally freed me from bulimia and OCD, and ultimately led me to the transforming Gospel of Jesus Christ. As Ryan stated in the dream, "Look at me! I have a new body!"

Estranging Novum. It is a curious thing how God saves us. But however it happens, even strange and mysterious as it may be, it is glorious.

Chapter 18
The Wilderness

But when they told him what had happened, he wouldn't believe them and said
that the White Stag was only a legend. Even despite Eve's miraculous recovery,
he wouldn't believe or go with them. So, Eve reluctantly took Jacob and Kate
and returned to the Forest of the Silver Birch because she knew it was right.
Indeed, it was there that she was finally released from the prison that held her
captive for so long. The prison that was her own mind.

The Queen's Doctor, *Brumbletide and the Queen's Doctor's Story*

The story of the Exodus in the Bible is probably my favorite of the whole thing. It is a perfect picture of the Gospel! The Israelites were slaves in Egypt. They could not get out. They could *want* to get out, but they could not get themselves out.

They needed a Savior.

Then Moses, the chosen one, went to tell Pharaoh to let God's people go. Not only did Pharaoh decline to let the Israelites go, but he made life much harder for them, causing them to think that perhaps Moses coming to get them wasn't a good thing after all.

Isn't that a picture of spiritual warfare? Spiritual adversaries of God love having slaves and do not want to lose them. They will fight like hell to stay our master. But nothing will keep God from bringing His people out of bondage when He hears their cries for salvation.

After many plagues, Pharaoh still refused to let the Israelites go. God then sent the tenth and final plague, the death of the firstborn son.

The Israelites were to slaughter an unblemished lamb and brush its blood on their door. They would then eat a special meal in haste while standing up, ready to go because God would miraculously bring them out of Egypt that very night. The Israelites did as God said, and when the angel of death came through Egypt that night, the firstborn son of anyone who did not have the blood of the lamb on their door was killed. But for those who did have the blood on their door, the angel of death passed them by.

We Christians have the blood of Jesus, the Lamb of God, on our door, and we are graciously and mercifully passed over in judgment.

After that plague, Pharaoh finally let the Israelites go, but when they left Egypt, he changed his mind, and he and his army chased them to the Red Sea. Where it seemed like everything had taken a turn for the worse and leaving Egypt was a mistake, where there seemed to be no way forward, God miraculously parted the sea, both letting the Israelites escape on dry ground and drowning the Egyptians as they went in after them trying to get them back. What a picture of the miraculous salvation of God! He brings His people out of the bondage of sin to this day, keeping them safe from spiritual adversaries and ensuring safe arrival in true life with Him.

We are free! We have seen miracles! God is real; there is no mistake. And He is loving and good. You want to run and yell it from the mountain tops!

And yet, like the Israelites, the wilderness is the next stop. It is wild and unfamiliar, and you do not know what the heck you are doing.

The time after my rebirth was both glorious and clumsy; I would also say downright embarrassing at times. I am used to being embarrassed, but I certainly don't enjoy it.

Coming from an extensive background in narcissism, I felt I was the only one who had truly experienced this New Creation in Christ. The good thing was that I was ready and willing to give the Gospel to anyone and everyone I met—but I was really annoying about it.

In my mind, no one *really* knew the Bible or the Gospel because I didn't hear anyone talking about how miraculous it was. If I hadn't been so engrossed in the Bible and getting to know this God who rescued me, I would have embarrassed myself much more than I did. I was blissfully ignorant until a few years down the road when it became apparent that there were, in fact, other true Christians on the planet, and quite a few of them at that.

There is a term for this early phase of transformation that I am convinced only the most ridiculous of us experience. "Cage Stage" is a period when you should be kept in a cage because, in your mind, you are ready to slay all the sinners in the world, but in reality, you are far from ready for anything. If anyone is slaying sinners, it isn't us, the sinners.

I still did—and do—stupid things as a New Creation too, like the time I decided to switch churches.

I had been attending a good church when all of this was happening. They had a good pastor, and the pastor's wife was wonderful to me. She took a lot of time with me when God was bringing me through the tumultuous change, and I still hold a special place for her in my heart. But while I loved her and was so grateful to her (and I still love her and am grateful for her), I felt the need to find a different church. I tried a few for a while but didn't find one that was any better than the one I was at.

But when I finished therapy, I knew Sarah Beth's husband was a pastor, and I had grown to love Sarah Beth immensely. I asked her if I could try out her church since she wasn't seeing me as a patient anymore. She said yes.

The first Sunday I visited River Hills Church, Sarah Beth was out of town. The sermon was about peace in the pasture of the Good Shepherd. "Peace in the pasture" was a phrase Sarah Beth and I constantly said throughout my therapy! It meant that

Jesus is the Good Shepherd, and we are safe and nourished in His pasture.

He makes me lie down in green pastures. He leads me beside still waters.

Psalm 23:2

Sarah Beth had told me that when the Bible said, "be still" it actually meant to "cease striving." I had been spinning my wheels to please God for months, but He was calling me to stop and listen to Him through His word. She also told me that Psalm 23 says, "He leads me beside still waters" because sheep will not drink from moving water. The Good Shepherd leads His sheep to where they will actually find refreshment. He had certainly refreshed me.

A large part of learning to deal with OCD is understanding that feelings, even strong ones, are not facts and are not to be followed before thorough examination. But it sure felt like God was saying through the pastor's Good Shepherd sermon, "This is it! This is the one!"

Then the pastor went on to state three big changes that would be coming to the church soon. His third announcement was that they would be starting a discipleship program, which was the number one thing I sought in a new church. I was sold.

I have been a member of River Hills for six years now, and it has been six years of wonderful. I have a group that reads and dissects Scripture every week. Strong discipleship has produced the most incredible Christians. I have seen God do so much in that church in the woods, which used to be a feed store for farm animals. It is still a place where people come for sustenance.

But, as I said, the clumsy was right there with the glorious. When I left the one church to go to the other, I wasn't mature about it. I sent a short text message and nothing else to the wonderful pastor's wife, who had been so kind and generous to me with her time. I still had so much growing to do. I still have so much growing to do! Thankfully, we can always rest in Romans 8:28. Everything, even my ignorant and blunderous moments, works together for the good of those who love God. My Cage Stage and the stupid things I do and say to this very day—all of it. But even amid the annoying and judgy Cage Stage and immaturity, my approach to others was still much better than it was before.

Even with all my mistakes and embarrassments, the words that come to mind when I think of new life in Christ are *contentment, joy,* and *treasure.*

In the wilderness, God sanctifies us, shedding our Old Self and revealing the New Self. In addition to my bumps and blunders, these past seven years have been riddled with disease, heartbreak, financial woes, infestations, death, disappointment, rejection—the list goes on. During the writing of this book, my husband, Jason, started experiencing tightness in his chest and is now scheduled for a stent to be put in his heart in two weeks.

Not only did most of those things happen before I was a Christian, but on this side of the fence, God has been faithful in growing and strengthening my faith and joy through all the hardships. He really does give you a peace that surpasses all understanding. Glory to God alone. Life with Christ is certainly an adventure, but what an incredible adventure it is, complete with excitement, terror, wonder, joy, worry, questioning, and the Treasure of the Universe.

Call to me and I will answer you and tell you great and unsearchable things you do not know.'

Jeremiah 33:3

Chapter 19
The End

Yet Bastian knew that he couldn't leave without the book. It was clear to him that he had only come to the shop because of this book. It had called him in some mysterious way, because it wanted to be his, because it had somehow always belonged to him.

Michael Ende, *The Neverending Story*

Thankfully, during my longer than necessary Cage Stage, God kept me busy by dropping a story into my head that had nowhere to go but out.

Even with all the grammatical errors and typos, I know I have a God-given gift for writing because it comes easily to me, I enjoy it, and people have been drawn to it since I was a kid.

My mother wrote stories, so not only did I watch her take time to sit at our family computer in the basement, smoke cigarettes, and write *Henrietta the Babycrib,* but she also made a point to encourage me to write. I am sure it is to her disdain that I always add that she smoked cigarettes while writing, but I do so because it is such an important detail. You do not need to have it all together to write. You do not have to be a professor or a theologian. You do not have to dress up or put on a happy face. You do not have to wait until you are through the valley. In fact, most of the time, the writing in the valley ends up being the best. Come as you are and pour out your soul.

So, because of Mom, I became good friends with pencils and paper. I started with poems because that is what we learned first in school. I loved to write limericks and still have a notebook full of them. Here is one I wrote when I was maybe ten:

A quarter past midnight,
All through the house,
Not a creature was stirring,
All except for one mouse.
Yes, there in the corner
With his tiny little head,
Was that mouse, that mouse named Fred.
"What's wrong, Fred? Why are you up?"
Said Fred, "I seem to have a case of the common hiccup.
I tried eating some sugar,
Which was very good,
But that didn't work,
Not like it should.
I tried holding my breath,
I turned very blue.
Hiccup! Hiccup!
Oh, what should I do?"
"Hey Fred, I have a clue.
I'll just sneak up behind you and give a big BOO!"
"Oh my, that gave me quite a fright.
Hey, my hiccups are gone,

I can sleep tonight!"
Oh good, now Fred is asleep,
Not making a sound or even a peep.
Hiccup! Hiccup!
Oh, how could it be?
Fred has given the hiccups to me!

An assignment on onomatopoeia in second grade sparked the notion that I wanted people to read what I wrote. The teacher chose a few of the poems written by us kids, wrote them in Sharpie on huge sheets of paper, and posted them on the wall. Mine was one. I was a star.

Then, I can't remember how old I was or what poem it was, but I won an award in elementary school. We dressed up and went to a high school in another city, where the fantastic children's book author Carmen Agra Deedy presented me with the award.

A funny side story: I had the pleasure of meeting Carmen Agra Deedy again at a library book event. I was starstruck. I gifted her my middle grade fantasy series, which she didn't ask for, to show her that I had blossomed as a writer since the award ceremony, which she, of course, wouldn't remember since it was thirty years ago. She was so kind and gladly accepted *Brumbletide.* But then, months later, I noticed an option on Amazon to buy my books used. When I looked, the used books had a picture included. Behold, there was my note to Carmen on the inside cover! A dagger to the heart. The lesson here is that if you force your work on someone, do not be surprised if you see it in a thrift store.

Back to ten-year-old Angie, it was also around this time that I became a reader. As a family, we were not readers, but my two best friends, Tina Chang and Anastasia Smith, were the kind of readers that would get so engrossed in a book that you had to shake them to snap out of it. I became a reader simply as a result of being their friend.

The first book I really loved was *Superfudge* by Judy Bloom. Then I discovered Beverly Clearly's Ramona books and could not get enough of them. Ramona and Beezus were so relatable! I was wowed by Roald Dahl's humor and over-the-top hideous villains. He is still one of my favorite authors to this day. I took inspiration from Dahl when crafting Margerie Prewitt and Queen Mother Maymie for *Brumbletide.*

In third grade, I specifically remember buying *Number the Stars* by Lois Lowry from the Scholastic Book Fair and reading the whole thing in both horror and intrigue.

When I was eleven or twelve, somehow, I ended up checking out a Sidney Sheldon book from the library—highly inappropriate for a tween. Of course, I couldn't put it down. I read it all and checked out the rest, blasting through every one. I wonder what the librarian thought of such a young kid checking out all those racy books. It's funny to think about.

But when the fourteenth birthday lunchroom incident happened, I exchanged reading library books for Cosmopolitan

Magazine and creative writing for painting my face and sculpting my body.

I was always a mediocre student but managed an A or B without trying in Language Arts. But being so self-absorbed as a teenager, especially when my parents divorced, even Language Arts suffered grade-wise. I got so behind in school, who knows what year I would have graduated. The series of unfortunate events continued for two decades. I didn't write anything except in diaries, which I do believe is still something. During this time, I rarely read anything but fitness magazines, but I did read one series of books, and they were very important. When I was nineteen, I worked briefly as a worthless receptionist at a granite and marble wholesaler. Terri, the God-send friend I met at Waffle House, introduced me to a book series she was reading called *Harry Potter*. I took *Harry Potter and the Sorcerer's Stone* to work with me and read the whole thing instead of working and did the same with the rest of the series published then. Needless to say, I did not stay employed there much longer. But I had become a massive fan of this fantastic story about wizards! The oasis in my literary desert that was *Harry Potter* stuck with me, and I went back to the wizarding world for a comforting escape during postpartum depression.

Shortly after having Ryan, I decided I wanted to try my hand at a fitness blog like the one I enjoyed by Julie Fagen called *Peanut Butter Fingers*. At that time, I was still identifying as a fitness enthusiast, living a healthy lifestyle about half the time and bingeing and purging the other half. I would blog for several days about my healthy eating and exercise routines and then not blog during the bulimic bouts. I have often wondered how many fitness bloggers have something similar going on behind the scenes.

I wrote that blog for six years. When the postpartum insanity started setting in, the posts got stranger and stranger. In the week after having the dream of Ryan and the snake, if something came into my mind that I thought was God, I did what it said. Unluckily for me, I thought almost every thought was from God that week. One particular day, I thought God was telling me to make a video with no makeup on, open the Bible, and read whatever I turned to. I did it and posted the weird video online. Thankfully, I had turned to Psalm 31, a beautiful passage, but the video was bizarre, nonetheless.

In you, Lord, I have taken refuge;
let me never be put to shame;
deliver me in your righteousness.
Turn your ear to me,
come quickly to my rescue;
be my rock of refuge,
a strong fortress to save me.
Since you are my rock and my fortress,
for the sake of your name lead and guide me.
Keep me free from the trap that is set for me,
for you are my refuge.
Into your hands I commit my spirit;
deliver me, Lord, my faithful God.

THE END

I hate those who cling to worthless idols;
as for me, I trust in the Lord.
I will be glad and rejoice in your love,
for you saw my affliction
and knew the anguish of my soul.
You have not given me into the hands of the enemy
but have set my feet in a spacious place.
Be merciful to me, Lord, for I am in distress;
my eyes grow weak with sorrow,
my soul and body with grief.
My life is consumed by anguish
and my years by groaning;
my strength fails because of my affliction,
and my bones grow weak.
Because of all my enemies,
I am the utter contempt of my neighbors
and an object of dread to my closest friends—
those who see me on the street flee from me.
I am forgotten as though I were dead;
I have become like broken pottery.
For I hear many whispering,
"Terror on every side!"
They conspire against me
and plot to take my life.
But I trust in you, Lord;
I say, "You are my God."
My times are in your hands;
deliver me from the hands of my enemies,
from those who pursue me.
Let your face shine on your servant;
save me in your unfailing love.
Let me not be put to shame, Lord,
for I have cried out to you;
but let the wicked be put to shame
and be silent in the realm of the dead.

Let their lying lips be silenced,
for with pride and contempt
they speak arrogantly against the righteous.
How abundant are the good things
that you have stored up for those who fear you,
that you bestow in the sight of all,
on those who take refuge in you.
In the shelter of your presence you hide them
from all human intrigues;
you keep them safe in your dwelling
from accusing tongues.
Praise be to the Lord,
for he showed me the wonders of his love
when I was in a city under siege.
In my alarm I said,
"I am cut off from your sight!"
Yet you heard my cry for mercy
when I called to you for help.
Love the Lord, all his faithful people!
The Lord preserves those who are true to him,
but the proud he pays back in full.
Be strong and take heart,
all you who hope in the Lord.

God still worked it out for the good. I did desperately need to hear that Scripture, after all. But God was doing much more than giving me words of comfort (which did not comfort me at the time). After a week of doing whatever popped into my mind in case it was God telling me to do it, I was even more curious about how God actually talks to us. If it was, in fact, through intrusive thoughts and intense feelings, walking with the Lord was going to drive me to suicide.

The year of the dream, God sorted me out. My fitness identity proved to be a flimsy one at best, so the "fitness" part of the blog faded away, as did my readers, whom I do not blame in the least. With fitness the least of my worries, I paid little to no attention to exercise and healthy eating. With my passion for fitness gone, when it came to the blog, all that was left was the writing.

Whether it was my thoughts, my sinking-sand lifestyle, or the things I was learning, I was compelled to write about it all, both privately and publicly.

Before making an appointment with Sarah Beth, I happened upon a YouTube video that was about obsessive-compulsive disorder, which I was starting to think might be something I was experiencing. A psychologist I saw for my disordered eating when I was a teenager said that she thought I had OCD, but I didn't believe her. I was far from wanting to be better back then. I didn't even want to be sitting in her office.

The doctor on the video was discussing OCD and a form of treatment for it called Exposure Response Prevention therapy, or ERP. This is where an individual, with the help of a trained therapist, exposes themselves to their obsessions in order to change pathways in the brain. Engaging in compulsions around the obsession temporarily relieves the anxiety but overall makes it worse. Exposure to the obsession, in turn, trains the brain that a person's fear around the obsession is invalid, and over time, the anxiety decreases. So, if someone has the most famous, yet widely misunderstood, kind of obsessive-compulsive disorder, contamination OCD, where they are extremely fearful of germs, the form of ERP they would exercise would be something like cleaning a toilet and not washing their hands immediately after.

Scrupulosity is a horribly named form of OCD where an individual is terrified God will punish them if they do not act out certain rituals or prayers. ERP for someone with this kind of OCD would maybe be to go to a cemetery or read a particular Bible passage that evokes that fear in them and then not engage in the ritual or prayer with the help of the therapist.

This concept is simple, but for the sufferer, the exercise is anything but. It is extremely taxing mentally and emotionally and should only be done with a professional. So, of course, I set out to do it alone. I did not want to have to go see someone, and I especially did not want to take medication. What if it made me even *more* crazy? I had no margin for that.

Since, at the time, my compulsions were primarily mental, I tried to think of ways I could face my fear of Ryan dying without the obvious. I thought writing about it might work since I felt strongly that my thoughts would manifest if I said them out loud or wrote them. This is called "magical thinking."

Another form of ERP was happening at this same time, and there was nothing I could do about it. In August of 2017, Ryan started school, something I had dreaded since I brought him home. I hated the thought of him being away from me for so long each day. That first day, I cried dropping him off. I cried all the while he was there. I counted the minutes that seemed like years until I could go get him. I cried for three days straight.

But on that first day, in my wash of tears, I exposed myself to the writing of his death. For some reason, I made it a fictional scene, probably because I thought it would be less painful. I made up the characters and the scenario, but I do not remember anything else about it except that I wrote it in a mess of sobs. That was my strange beginning in fiction novel writing. Those characters and that scene never made it into any story except this one, but shortly after that, I had a vision of a woman who would become Lenore in *Brumbletide* telling the protagonist, who was a boy at the time, "We are all royals here" in a room filled with thrones and people dressed like kings and queens. It was inspired by my many years of thinking I was a Christian, acting and dressing like one, telling myself how special I was because I was God's creation, but I was actually not a true Christian at all because I had not entered through the correct Door.

I am the door. If anyone enters by me, he will be saved and will go in and out and find pasture.

John 10:9

I was so close to the truth but had missed it completely. What if there was a whole building of people like that? There was a story there, and it was in my head, and I had to get it out, or I'd burst.

C.S. Lewis calls his *Chronicles of Narnia* a "supposal" as opposed to an allegory. *Suppose* there was a place called Narnia in need of redemption. How would that play out? I decided I would like my story to be a supposal too. With those basics established, I started writing. Day after day, while Ryan was at school, I went to the paper to see what would show up on it. This happened for weeks and then months until one day, there it was: THE END.

Chapter 20
Brumbletide

We Prewitts enjoy the finer things in life. Tonight, for instance, we are dining in the living room by the light of a horror flick Dad's wanted to see. We are enjoying a delicious meal of chickenless nuggets, mac-n-cheese product, and cubed vegetables. Mum's specialty is frozen dinners so, believe it or not, we have them most nights.

Maggie Prewitt, *Brumbletide and the Daughter of Eve*

Brumbletide is a story about a small town, average in every way except for a gigantic magic castle that floats in the sea right beside it. The general public, young and old, rich and poor, go there to be treated like royalty. But while this castle lavishes its guests with the finest and wows them with magical happenings, it turns out to be a sinister knock-off of a true and good kingdom that is hidden from the people literally beneath the masquerade.

The inspiration for this idea came because I now knew that one could think they were a Child of God and heir to the Kingdom, but it was quite possible that they were not, and there were also those who knew perfectly well they were not Children of God but were out to deceive. They may dress the part and act the part but are further from the Kingdom than atheists because the best lies are those closest to the truth. But no matter how dark the darkness, how evil the evilness, there is always hope for the hopeless.

I finished the first version of *Brumbletide* in 2018, but it was very different from what it is now. It was called *Godspeed*. Pippin the White Stag king was a winged horse named something even I have a hard time pronouncing. It was almost an entirely different book except for the premise that it was about a castle where the general public came to be treated like royalty.

I got the manuscript as good as I could get it at the time, which those of you who have read *Brumbletide* can imagine how horrific the grammar errors and typos were.

"What?" She said.

It looked right to me back then to capitalize the word after a quotation. I have since learned many things about punctuation. Some of it still doesn't look right to me, so I simply don't do it. I do not recommend doing this for your own book.

When you want to publish a book traditionally, you have to get a literary agent. It is the literary agent who then pitches your book to publishing houses. Getting a literary agent is *not* the same as getting a real estate agent. Real estate agents bend over backward to get you to choose them to sell your house. Not so with literary agents. You first have to send them a query letter about your book and why it might benefit them. If they like the idea of your story, they then ask for a few chapters. If they like those, then they will request the full manuscript. After a lot of reading on their part, which takes a lot of time because your manuscript is only one of many, if they like your story and think they might be able to sell it, they will offer you representation. If they do not believe it will be good for them, they send a rejection email. More often than not, the author gets a rejection.

I queried many agents for *Godspeed* and received almost as many immediate rejections as I sent out queries. That is when I rewrote the book, which turned out to be for the best. I rewrote the whole thing, and by the end, I knew this was the story I was meant to write.

It was now 2019, and I was back in the query trenches, but this time, I was querying *Brumbletide*, and this time I got an agent! *Brumbletide* then went on submission to publishing houses which I will talk about in my chapter about publishing. This chapter is all about how *Brumbletide* became what it is. I am beginning with this part about querying literary agents because the most important character, Pippin, did not come until after I was on submission to agents.

Pippin, the White Stag king of *Brumbletide,* is my Christ-type in the story. But until I was re-reading *The Lion the Witch and the Wardrobe* after I had already gotten my agent, Pippin was the white winged horse. I think I might have changed his name to Pippin already at that time. Maybe not.

But one night I was reading Chapter 14 of the first book in *The Chronicles of Narnia*, The Hunting of the White Stag. The white stag is not C.S. Lewis's creation, it has been a creature of mythology for centuries. Though I had read the chapter before, something struck me about the mysterious stag this time.

What if this white stag is an appearing Aslan? What if he is leading the Pevensie children out of Narnia for his own purposes? What if he has other kingdoms?

I changed the winged horse to the White Stag, and there I had my Pippin. I knew there might be many people who didn't like the idea of a deer as the Christ-type instead of a lion. Any time you set your pen to an endeavor such as writing a Christ-type, criticism will come. But when does criticism not come? And if fear of criticism is keeping you from writing the story that has come into your mind, I am sorry to say you will never be the author of anything worth reading.

However, when writing a Christ-type, I have concluded that it is better to write a faulty Christ-type than not to write one at all. In the Bible, we have Adam, Moses, Joseph, and Jonah, to name a few men full of sin that God used to draw everyone's eyes to the perfect Messiah of Jesus. So, not only do I know that all things, even a fantasy story written by a woman who has the English and grammar skills of a sixth grader, will work to the good of those who love God (Romans 8:28), but I also know that it is better to attempt to write a Christ-type that perhaps God will use to point three people to Jesus's door than to write a novel that has no such character.

But why a stag and not something better like a mighty lion? Well, for one, the lion was taken by C.S. Lewis, and I actually do have what I think is good reason for the stag. Here, I state my case!

Take my yoke upon you, and learn from me, for I am gentle and lowly in heart, and you will find rest for your souls.

Matthew 11:29

Contrary to what anyone expected, Jesus was humble and lowly of heart from His birth until He graciously died for us and then rose in glory. He was born in a manger and announced first to shepherds instead of kings. His triumphal entry was on a donkey, and his moment of purpose was a bloody and humiliating death on a cross. When He rose again, he did so quietly, only telling Mary Magdalene until he met his friends and informed them as well. This is our King, the treasure of the universe.

My beloved is like a gazelle or a young stag. Behold, there he stands behind our wall, gazing through the windows, looking through the lattice.

Song of Solomon 2:9

As the miracle of the water to wine displays, Jesus came to marry His Church. A wedding was going to occur, the Old Covenant would be no more, and a New Covenant would take its place. The book of Song of Solomon is a beautiful love song between two lovers. As Christ came to marry His Church, we can imagine his longing and excitement for His Love in the time until the ceremony, which was His death and resurrection. It was then that the Old was gone, and the New had come! In Jesus and the Holy Spirit, God now dwelt with His people again.

He made my feet like the feet of a deer and set me secure on the heights.
2 Samuel 22:34

This Old Testament verse rings true when we are made into a New Creation in Christ. When the Gospel is planted in good soil in our hearts, we are done, destroyed, and then resurrected as a New Creation that Jesus conforms daily to be like Himself. This is wonderful news for us and is the light of the world. Even in this dark world of suffering, we are set on the heights. Even in our suffering, we somehow endure in peace. And when we do not have peace in our suffering, we know that if we are one of these New Creations, the suffering is for a good and perfect purpose, even if beyond our understanding. As we walk through the valley of the shadow of death, we do not have to fear, for His rod and staff comfort us.

Brumbletide is flawed. Pippin is flawed. But my goal in writing the story was and is to present a picture of our mess, both caused by others and our own, and in a fantastical way show the redemption of it all in a way that points to the door of Jesus Christ.

So there. I may or may not have convinced you, but now you know how Pippin came about.

You may be thinking all that sounds fine, but of all things, why a children's fantasy? And why one that has so much death and darkness?

I heard once that when a person becomes an addict, their brain pauses development past the age that they are at the time. I have no idea if that is true or not, but if it is, maybe that is why I love middle grade fiction. While I do love children's stories to this day, all I can say as to why *Brumbletide* is a middle grade fiction is that the vision of Lenore that fell into my head that day had the air of a children's fantasy, and so that is what it had to be. Why so much death? Well, what I had to say in the story involved a lot of death. When we veer from God in the slightest, there is death. As the Proverb says, there is a way that seems right to man but, in the end, leads to death. And not just the eventual death of ourselves but the death of the innocent.

I didn't plan the story to go that way; it just did. When it comes to writers, there are plotters and pantsers. Plotters plan and plot the whole story in advance before writing it. Pantsers fly by the seat of their pants when it comes to their story. They do not outline anything; they begin writing and see what emerges. I am a pantser all the way. The magical creatures in *Brumbletide*, the Snickerlings and warmouths, were not pre-planned at all. I found them in my head as I wrote this story about royals, and there they were. But after they were crafted, I thought they might bring angels and cherubim to mind. The death of the Snickerlings to fuel the magic of Emily Castle, in my mind, is like abortion or human trafficking.

Brumbletide, Pippin's almost empty kingdom, would be the true kingdom of God. Hopefully, by the end of the series, it will have a few more people in it.

The Dragon is the ancient serpent deceiver. Michelle is the antichrist. He is killed at the end of the first book, but since he has infected the whole kingdom and lives on in the hearts of not only Emily royals but all of Little Ipswich, much work remains.

Maggie and her family represent the average household. The mother is over-the-top horrible, but we all know someone vicious like that, and while it may not be a wicked mother, more households than not have something dark going on in them. Also, more households than not are messy like the Prewitts. They are not what they portray on social media; they do not have it together, and there are many families who aren't actually raising their children but only letting them wander until they are grown. These are the children I want *Brumbletide* to connect with, and those hopeless, misunderstood, and ashamed for whatever reason. And I do mean *whatever the reason.* They can see themselves in Maggie and see where Pippin takes her. An underdog who doesn't even belong in the game falls face-first and clumsily into heroism.

Pippin's seven Chosen represent the aspects of life that make for an enjoyable society and also how God, through Jesus, restores us to our proper purpose. They each have a tower at both

Brumbletide and Emily, and their specific vocations are the classes taught at the academy.

Justice, a former alcoholic, brings hospitality to the kingdom.

Sara Lisa, formerly seeking attention from men, brings beauty and celebration.

George, formerly an instrument of holocaust, becomes a righteous master of sport.

Flori, a thief, now *gives* life as she plants and tends the Hanging Gardens.

The twins, Soleil and Michelle, sun and moon, are both academically brilliant. Soleil is a scientist and mathematician. Michelle is a historian and master of language. While their former way of life is left to interpretation, Soleil chooses to follow Pippin and help him rule his kingdom, while Michelle is skeptical, and though he follows in the beginning, in the end, he rebels, deceives, and chooses to find a way to have his own extravagant kingdom where he alone is king.

Eve, formerly insane, is the queen of wisdom.

Then there are little hidden gems throughout the series. The celebration of Cervi Day at the castle is a play on the scientific name for deer, Cervidae. The Queen's Doctor in the fourth book is C.S. Lewis. Several of the Emily Academy students are named after my own friends.

This is not a hidden gem because I certainly didn't know it would occur. *Brumbletide and the Changing of the Crowns* was published exactly one year to the day before Queen Elizabeth died, and there actually was a changing of the crowns.

This story is as much for me as it is for anyone else. These are thoughts that I had rolling around in my mind that had to be sorted. It just so happened they were sorted into children's fantasy novels about magical royals.

Chapter 21
The Gift of Humiliation

My first class is Hoplology with Atticus and Thorn. We are freezing—absolutely freezing. The weather is frosty, and we are all gathered on carpets in midair in front of Queen Mother Berthilda. Two or so dozen young royals are bundled in white furs and huddled two or three to a carpet held by Snickerlings. The magical flying children are dressed in no more than their usual patchwork attire and seem unfazed by the cold.

Four Snickerlings hold Queen Mother Berthilda's carpet in front of the others while she raises her large arms to get everyone's attention.

"Hear, hear! Attention, your majesties! As many of you know, the one hundred and seventy-fifth Em Games are right around the corner. In preparation, we will be performing exercises more daring than usual. We break the ice today with Tower Climbing."

Gasps escape from around the carpets. Even the Snickerlings appear a little worried and lean in to whisper what I gather to be consoling words to their passengers.

"Now, now, not to worry, class. You will be monitored the whole time, and if you happen to fall, Snickerlings will come to your rescue immediately. Any questions?" Queen Mother Berthilda scans the class.

"Has anyone died before?" shouts Eden Kung over the wind.

Berthilda considers his question as if she isn't sure whether to answer honestly. "Yes, some have. None in the past few years though."

There have been no games in recent years! The last were twelve years ago!

"And if the worst should happen, what a way to go, eh?" The Queen Mother flashes a toothy smile reciprocated by no one. "Right. Now, everyone, do your very best—especially you, Champions. Let this not be the year we break our Triad winning streak."

"Yeah!" shouts Atticus. "Let's do it, Champs!" A few other Champions whistle and applaud as well.

Meanwhile, I haven't gotten past the name of the event—Tower Climbing. My head is back as far as it will go as I take in the massive monstrosity that is George Tower. It can't mean what it sounds like, can it?

"For those of you unaware," pipes Queen Mother Berthilda, "Tower Climbing is exactly as it sounds. You will be climbing George Tower."

Pushing Thorn out of the way, I lean over and puke off the side of the carpet into the Lux below.

"Maggie!" shouts Atticus. "Are you alright?"

I sit back up woozily. "No."

"Blimey," mumbles Thorn, checking her gown for vomit.

Atticus nudges my shoulder and whispers, "Heights are my greatest fear, but I'm going to suck it up and go first since I'll be leading the Em Games and all." He raises his hand.

"Yes, Prince Atticus? Oh, are you alright, Princess Maggie? You're green."

I lean over and puke again.

"Eesh, let's trade places," says Thorn, crawling to the center of the carpet.

Atticus waits a second to show a little concern but no longer. "I volunteer to go first, Queen Mother Berthilda."

"How wonderful. Your carpet can come forward then."

To my horror, the Snickerlings fly us to the ledge at the bottom of George Tower. A large stone winged hound—George's warmouth—sits at the corner permanently fixed on Little Ipswich.

Queen Mother Berthilda's carpet hovers next to ours.

"Our brilliant ancestor, King George, designed his tower to be climbed. There are grooves all around it for your hands and feet. The things to overcome are

the wind, your lack of strength, and, of course, your own fear. Prince Atticus, godspeed."

Without hesitation, Atticus grabs hold of the hound and pulls himself onto the ledge. He catches a glimpse of the Lux far down below on his way, and a flash of panic sweeps his face. But without closing his eyes, he takes a deep breath and stands up straight. Immediately, he begins climbing fast up the tower. His small frame is of benefit to him here. He stumbles once, and Snickerlings lunge forward, but he immediately regains his footing and continues upward at an impressive pace. Before long, Atticus has made it halfway up the tower and waves to us from what is certainly two hundred feet in the air.

"Bravo! Bravo, Prince Atticus! And a Champion, no less," Queen Mother Berthilda shouts gleefully.

Snickerlings soar to Atticus and bring him down safely to our carpet. In the snowy wind, he is sweaty and out of breath.

He swats the air. "Wasn't anything. A nice warm-up."

Thorn is next. She doesn't seem happy about the task but not terrified either. Quietly, she steps onto the ledge and is smart enough not to look down. Not so quickly as Atticus, but at a decent pace, she climbs the tower.

"Steady, calculated, precise— the Firebreather way," Berthilda tells us quietly as if not to disturb Thorn's concentration.

Eventually, Thorn reaches the halfway point and raises her hand.

"Well done, Princess Thorn!" Berthilda shouts as Snickerlings fly her to the carpet.

"Next we have—" She pauses because I'm apparently still green. "Princess Maggie."

I hoist my body, which seems to weigh a ton, onto the ledge and cling for dear life to the wings of the stone hound. I feel woozy and, without meaning to, catch a glimpse of how high I am. Puke immediately projects into the air and makes its way into the carpets holding my classmates who squeal in disgust. I close my eyes and breathe, trying to compose myself, and when I feel the first bit of relief, turn and mount the tower.

Atticus and Thorn have deceived me. Even pulling myself onto the tower takes all my strength, and my arms are already burning as I hold myself up. The flag marking halfway up the tower seems a mile high. I'll never make it. I won't even make it five grooves in. I let go of a groove and immediately grab the next closest. My legs and arms are trembling, and my body is getting heavier by the second. I've never been athletic—how am I going to do this? Atticus and Thorn must have done this before. Yes, of course, they have!

With my arms already so fatigued that I can't raise a hand, I yell, "I can't do it! My arms are giving out!"

In a blink of an eye, I am in the arms of Snickerlings and then back with Thorn and Atticus on the carpet. I don't feel that ashamed when Queen Mother Berthilda doesn't give me a "good try" or anything, but little do I know the shame will grow heavier and heavier as every single student climbs high onto the tower. Even Eden, whose fear had him crying on his way up, made it to the flag. I alone was the only one not strong enough to do it.

And I am supposed to be the Head of Emily Castle. Pathetic.

J. Reese Bradley, Brumbletide and the Triad Champion

I have come to believe that once you have been humiliated enough, the possibilities in life are endless. The world is your oyster when you couldn't care less what anyone thinks.

From as far back as I can remember, I was self-conscious, and I am sure it is my narcissism that tells me I was more self-conscious than most.

In daycare, I was heartbroken by a boy I didn't know because he came up to me and said, "I don't love you!" I had never seen the boy before in my short life, but he didn't love me! What had I done?

In sixth grade, I was in the rollerblading relay for Olympic Day. I loved rollerblading but had never had to measure up against others while doing it. When the races began, I quickly fell to last place where I stayed for the duration. I huffed and panicked my way around the football field while my classmates quite literally looked down on me from the stands.

Olympic Day never seemed to agree with me, nor could I seem to escape it. It followed me to camp the summer after the infamous eighth grade year. I hated summer camp anyway. It never failed that everyone was asleep before I was, leaving me in the dark, quiet cabin in the woods to ruminate on the apocalypse. But hearing that we were having an Olympic Day at camp wasn't as bad of news as usual because I was now physically fit. I exercised all the time—bring on the rollerblade relay! The only event I did not want to be a part of was the swim relay. Not only did I not want to be in a bathing suit, but I hated having anything in my eyes, including water. I am still like this, and I don't know why. Surely, of all the events, I would not get stuck with that one.

We were all gathered for signups when my friend who always seemed to be on her period told me to go back to the cabin with her so she could remedy her situation. I people-pleased, and when we returned, there was only one event left to choose. You guessed it—the swim relay.

I wasn't looking forward to swimming at all, and yet again, everyone would be looking down on me. They'd be looking down on me from the side of the pool! Was it too much to ask to at least embarrass myself on a level plane? But the time had come. I was last in line, and my team was the last lane of the pool. I paid no attention to the other swimmers or anything for that matter. I wanted to be as far removed from it all as possible. Way too soon, I was at the front of the line waiting for my teammate to tag my hand.

Tag.

I dove in and swam as fast as I possibly could—and I was fast! Losing weight had really improved my swim. Maybe this wasn't going to be so bad after all. Suddenly, someone smacked my head. Taken aback, I decided not to let it get me behind and plowed full steam ahead until I then smacked another swimmer on the back. I could tell by her feet kicking water all over the place that she was about to kick me too. What in the world? Determined, I kept going. I swam and swam and swam—and swam. I was so proud to be doing so well. Is this what it was like to be an athlete?

After what seemed like forever, I finally touched the other end of the pool. I stood up and wiped my eyes, which I hadn't opened the whole time. Remember, I hate anything in my eyes, even water.

It took me a minute to really see what I was seeing. I was looking up from the pool at every other camper. Everyone who had done the swim relay was already out of the pool, bundled in towels. Everyone was laughing hysterically. I was alone in the pool, and I alone was the only one to have swam exactly diagonally across all the lanes.

This story is hilarious, and I am laughing as I write it now, but you can imagine how *not* funny it was when I was fourteen. After the humiliation of the swim relay blunder, I went back to the cabin and for once hoped the world actually would come to a cataclysmic end.

Sports were always like this for me. I was so bad at them, except for figure skating. Oddly enough, I was really good at that and did it for years after the Atlanta Ice Forum was built by my house, of all places. A strange sport for a southern girl.

School was another horror story. I remember a teacher once saying this to the class, "The math tests are back. They range from ninety-four to nineteen."

Yes, I got the nineteen. I wish that was the worst I'd done on a test. I wouldn't pay attention to anything, always off in another world. But I was well-behaved and didn't draw any attention to the fact that I was a million miles away.

I was always lost in math, but at least I could be horrible at it in private. Oral reports were the nightmare of nightmares. I always hated standing up in front of the class for anything, but after the birthday lunchroom incident, I was crippled with fear of talking in front of my peers. After that, whenever I stood up to do an oral report, I cried. I *loathed* that I cried. It was certainly not by choice. I wasn't sad, I was anxious. But for some reason, tears would come, and I couldn't stop them. It was so frustrating and embarrassing. The last thing I needed was crying while trying to get through a report in front of the class. The crying response continued at school and jobs until I saw Sarah Beth at thirty-four.

Throughout the bulimic years, I was either heavy or thin. It seemed that no matter how heavy I was, the shame of it was a thousand times heavier. When I was thin, I wasn't confident then either. If anyone said anything about my appearance, good or bad, I picked it apart. *Do they really think I'm pretty? Or do they want me to continue to look this way so that I don't upstage them?* I thought things like that because that is how I was toward others. I didn't want them to upstage me.

Dropping out of high school to run away from my problems was humiliating because not only did I have no clue how to navigate the real world like I was so sure that I did, but I still had many problems, and now I had to wear a breakfast-colored uniform every day too.

I had shown everyone I knew and loved, and a bunch I didn't know and love, that I could not cut it in school, and I could not cut it in the real world. I couldn't even keep my weight down, the one thing I had been praised for at one time. I went on to not cut it in finances, marriage, or even displaying some semblance of sanity.

The point of this chapter is not to wallow even more in my failures. The point is that all of these years of humiliation, of which I only included a short list here, God worked together for good. After the radical rescue in 2017, when I was a New Creation less focused on my shortcomings and tallgoings, all of this falling through the mud went on to make the road to publishing a piece of cake. Oh, publishing was difficult, certainly. You are putting your work out there, waiting, getting rejected, waiting some more, getting rejected some more, and that is all before your book is actually published, where it is then subject to a whole new kind of scrutiny.

Rejection, rejection, rejection is the name of the publishing game whether you end up with a book deal or not. But at that point in my life, I had been humiliated so many times, and it was the kind of humiliation where you really let people down. There are times you say or do silly things that you wish you didn't, and then there is the kind of humiliation where you end up causing harm or disappointment to others because of your actions. I had *really* disappointed people I cared about. I even had a fair amount of public humiliation where I wanted to change my name and move to the woods—and I hate the woods. In comparison, rejection from literary agents and editors was nothing. I've known so many writers who shelved their book after only a few rejections. I would have certainly done the same, but everything works together for the good of those who love God. And God worked my humiliation together for my good in publishing and ultimately in living authentically in general.

I would like to end this chapter with one more embarrassing and funny story. This one happened when I was an adult, had already been made into a New Creation and yet, there I was still doing stupid things like this. And spoiler alert, it hasn't stopped.

The year was 2020. There was talk of a virus, but it had not made its way, we thought, to the U.S. I was dropping Ryan off for school, when all of us received a Tornado WARNING alert on our phones. I saw the alert, and then immediately one of women who was helping kids out of their cars, opens the door and exclaims, "Tornado warning! Get in the building!"

It was early. I listened. I shut off the car, got out, and ran into the building with Ryan. The next thing I knew, I was sitting in a hall with a bunch of chatty fifth graders and Ryan, who was only four. I looked and smelled like a homeless person since I had not gotten dressed for the day or even brushed my teeth. But that was okay. At least we were safe. Where were the other parents?

In a few minutes, a voice came over the intercom, "Will the driver of a grey Ford Explorer please move your vehicle out of the drop-off lane."

It was mine. When I went outside, there was my car that I had vacated and left in the drop-off lane with a line of cars behind it waiting in a Tornado Warning to drop of their child and find safety. I sheepishly moved my car to a parking space and went back inside to the fifth-grade hallway. Thank God the tornado never came, and I wasn't the cause of mass devastation. But it was another embarrassment for the books.

Joking aside, the next time you royally embarrass yourself, it will not feel good. You may even stay in bed for a few days recovering. But *really* feel it. Live in it. Make yourself at home in it. Tell yourself it will not be the last time. You must get used to the feeling because it is only after a multitude of these humiliating moments that you will then be ready to take on the world.

Chapter 22
Publishing

"Turn back, turn back, young maiden dear,
'Tis a murderer's house you enter here."
The Brothers Grimm, *The Robber Bridegroom*

Shortly after I joined River Hills Church in 2018, I was greeting at the door with a man named Wade Carey. We were cordial to one another but didn't speak much. I heard him talking to another man about a book he was reading. We went to the service. That was that.

Later that day both my husband and I received a friend request on Facebook from Wade. When I looked at his page, I was shocked to see this big guy in the trucking industry had authored nine books! Some were fiction, some were non-fiction, all were beautifully crafted, and I was in disbelief at what I was seeing. Were these his? There his name was on all the covers.

At that point, I had a completed manuscript that I was getting ready to send to agents. I am pretty sure the only thing I had posted about writing at that point was that I had written a book under a pseudonym, and that is why I was changing the name of my The Keen Peach blog page to J. Reese Bradley. As C.S. Lewis says, some of these facts are probably incorrect. It is not that authors want to lie to you. It is just that when it is all happening, we are busy living it and not thinking of what we will tell people after the fact. The most important detail at this time is that I had written a book that wasn't published yet, and Wade saw this on my Facebook page.

I commented on the picture of his books with, "You didn't say you *wrote* books!"

Wade replied, "I think we have a lot to talk about."

We met one morning in the church office. Wade was very kind and respectful, yet matter-of-a-fact and to-the-point, treating the get-together much like a business meeting. He gave me all the publishing information imaginable, but he wanted nothing in return. A new concept for me.

"I think I am supposed to show you how to publish," he said.

I thanked him. It just so happened that I wanted him to show me how.

For that hour, Wade walked me through how to self-publish books both beautifully and affordably.

This was obviously from the hand of God. I knew God had introduced Wade and me at the church door that morning. I knew God set up this meeting. I was so thankful to God for sending Wade to tell me how to self-publish—that is, if traditional publishing didn't work out.

Remember, I was a failure in life. Finishing a manuscript was a huge accomplishment for me since I had literally finished nothing else. I wanted to try to traditionally publish it. I wanted the publishing houses to tell me it was good. I thanked Wade, we remained in touch, and I set out on a traditional publishing journey that took the next two years.

The first of the two years was spent querying agents for *Godspeed*, getting immediate and ample rejection, re-writing the story that became *Brumbletide and the Daughter of Eve*, and then receiving more rejection.

The first time I received a request from an agent, it was from an agency called Pippin Properties. I was overcome with excitement. I knew this was from God. They had Pippin in their name, after all! Not only did Pippin Properties reject the manuscript, but I humiliated myself yet again. I had done my research about how to query agents, but I did not know that, as a rule, they did not get back to you for several months or that you are not supposed to bother them in the meantime. I bothered them in the meantime. A lot. They rejected the manuscript three months later.

The year-long journey to getting an agent was filled with hope, waiting, fantasizing, frustration, rejection, more rejection, more hope and fantasizing, and more frustration. Then, on the night of August 30th, we went to our friend's house to watch football. Since I am not a football fan, I was looking at my phone often. I checked my email. I couldn't believe my eyes. Marisa Zeppieri from Strachan Literary Agency had offered representation of *Brumbletide!* We all cheered, and our sweet friends opened a bottle of champagne to celebrate. I thanked God. Maybe He was with me on this traditional publishing journey, after all. It was starting to seem like He wasn't.

In October, *Brumbletide* went on submission to publishing house editors. It is the editors that read your manuscript and offer a book deal or not. It works the same way as querying agents, only this time, your agent queries the publishing houses and represents you. We were ecstatic when all of the big publishers requested *Brumbletide*. The children's divisions of Harper Collins, Simon and Schuster, and Chronicle were just some of the houses that wanted to read my work. When Bloomsbury requested, I prayed they would be the one because it was Bloomsbury who published my favorite series of all time, *Harry Potter*.

We waited. The wait time for a response was the same as for agents. I had learned not to bother the agents while waiting, and thankfully now I couldn't because Marisa was handling everything. But I did follow the editors on social media and subscribed to Publisher's Marketplace where you can see every book deal that is made. By September of 2020, I was so furious with the traditional publishing world, I wouldn't have agreed to a deal if they offered.

In the next paragraphs, I am going to make political and controversial statements. It is important to know that politics is not why *Brumbletide* did not get a book deal in the end. I can only guess why the editors that rejected *Brumbletide* did so because the rejections mostly had good things to say. I remember one, Chronicle I think, didn't like the story's voice. Understandable. But mostly, the reason was that it just wasn't for them. I'm sure they didn't like it. Understandable. But while God's plan for *Brumbletide* was not to be traditionally published, God did show me what was really going on in the publishing world. And it was dark.

All the while *Brumbletide* was being requested and read, these same editors were spewing their extreme liberal views on their social media platforms. *Brumbletide* happened to be on submission from October of 2019 until September of 2020. The Coronavirus pandemic mania was in full swing, and the nation all but divided when the murder of George Floyd happened in May. My manuscript was with a few editors at the time, but it was Bloomsbury's editor that I was paying the most attention to because I wanted her to be the one. But the more she posted on Twitter (it was Twitter then), the more I knew in my heart there was no way this woman would be offering me, a white conservative Christian, a book deal.

After George Floyd, I watched as she and the other editors tweeted that they were prioritizing books by black authors to amplify their voices. This is not the "dark" I mentioned. I love black authors, and I want them to have book deals, but this meant I was not in the running.

But I wasn't in the running anyway. Both literary agents and publishing house editors have the kinds of things they are looking for in a manuscript listed on their website and they also will tweet about it. There was one common request—Diverse Books.

I remember querying agents and constantly seeing "diverse" in their list, so in my query letter, I said that *Brumbletide* was diverse. I had included all kinds of races and classes in the story, after all. This seems silly now, but what I didn't know back then was that, according to the traditional publishing world, my book was far from diverse. Diverse Books have non-binary or transgender children with two dads or two moms or at least a gay uncle. If the book does not have these criteria, then the author certainly lives out loud as a liberal and promotes Diversity and Inclusion in literature at least every now and then.

Where is my proof of this, you ask? On Twitter and Publisher's Marketplace. You can go back and see everything said and every children's book deal made and decide for yourself. But the bottom line is that before taking the traditional publishing journey that I did, I had no idea the books that are available to our children in bookstores, book fairs, and libraries are either Diverse or written by a liberal author whose content is going to reflect that.

Why is this a problem, you ask? Everyone has their views. That does not mean they do not make great stories. I am with you. I fell in love with reading because of *Superfudge* by Judy Blume who is a liberal, and I am a huge fan of Lois Lowry who is too. Many of my favorite authors are far-left liberals. But there is something evil at large in recent years. Namely, the ideologies that boys can be girls and vice versa, gender fluidity, non-binary, and even humans can be animals if they want.

This is not a Right vs Left argument, this a good vs evil argument. Something out there is trying to erase man and woman, masculine and feminine, boy and girl. Rid a society of natural boundaries, and soon it will no longer be a civilization. Boundaries are what keeps chaos at bay, and without natural boundaries in place, humanity falls into chaos.

I am not going to go deep into Democrat vs Republican here, but I will say that it has gotten to the point that both Democrats and Republicans have set lists of ideologies they champion. Republicans are pro-vaccine choice, pro-life, pro-gun, and want closed borders. Democrats are vaccinated, pro-abortion, pro-gun control, and want bridges, not walls.

There is a ton of groupthink going on, and it will do us all well to heed Solomon's warning:

> *It is good to grasp the one and not let go of the other.*
> *Whoever fears God will avoid all extremes.*
>
> Ecclesiastes 7:18

But there is a difference between the above viewpoints and the ideology that boys can be girls and vice versa. These kinds of beliefs go against basic biology and are ruining young lives as children are given puberty blockers and sex-change surgeries. I foresee an angry generation of adults abused in childhood in the near future. And they certainly should be.

I digress. After a year on submission, I decided to withdraw my manuscript from the editors it was with and self-publish *Brumbletide.* At this point, I was in love with the idea of self-publishing. Not only had Wade so graciously sat me down two years earlier and convinced me it was a viable option, but I followed many successful self-published authors of fantastic books! When a friend of mine with a massive following shocked everyone by self-publishing her book, it sealed the deal for me that the self-publishing stigma was something of the past. Wade and I met again. He introduced me to the talented cover designer and book formatter, Rachel Bostwick, and the publishing ball was rolling.

It was Halloween night. We were at a neighbor's house getting ready to take the kids trick-or-treating when I received the cover of *Brumbletide and the Daughter of Eve.* It took my breath away. It was perfect—magical! On November 10th, 2020, *Brumbletide and the Daughter of Eve* was released to the public. It was the first in the *Brumbletide* series, and the second, *Brumbletide and the Changing of the Crowns,* was almost finished since I had been writing it all the while on submission. Everything was bliss for one year.

Chapter 23
Oops

And then, from the other room, we could hear Fudge singing himself to sleep. "M-a-i-n-e spells Maine. F-u-d-g-e spells Fudgie. P-e-t-e-r spells Pee-tah. B-e-e-r spells whiskey.

Judy Blume, *Superfudge*

The first year of being a published author was magical. My friends and family poured out support for me and the book. I had my first book event at the best bookstore in the world, The Story Shop, where the event was held in their magical storytime room. The entrance to it was a Narnian wardrobe, and you went through the wardrobe, coats, and all!

I had another event at a lovely bookstore called Liberty Books, which became my favorite place to hold events. For four hours, I stood at a table talking to anyone and everyone who walked by about everything under the sun. My dream job! I loved every minute. I sold out of my stock both times. The reviews started coming in: five stars, four stars, and the occasional three stars. This is normal when most of your readers who are reviewing your book are your friends and family. It wasn't until *Brumbletide and the Changing of the Crowns* was about to release that my blissful ignorance was about to come to an end.

I made a friend, Shannon. She was the David to my Jonathan. It isn't very common that you meet a woman who wants to talk about mother and wifehood, fashion and make-up, *and* theology and the esoteric. Shannon was immediately supportive of *Brumbletide* and began reading.

"Your editor has missed some things," she told me.

My editor was me.

For five years, I had read through and edited that book backward and forward. When I decided to self-publish, I gave it one more good read through and sent it off for formatting. The book was full of typos and grammatical errors.

While I had learned a lot about grammar and punctuation, I hadn't learned enough, and this was in addition to the fact that I had taken almost no time away from the manuscript. I was too close to the story and, therefore, rendered blind to many mistakes. This is true. If you are a writer, it is crucial to take at least a few weeks away from looking at your manuscript so that you can come back to it with fresh eyes.

I was horrified. The book had been like that for a year!

But thank God, humiliation was something I was a pro at. I decided to fix the book and re-release it at a special price along with *Changing of the Crowns*.

I scoured the manuscript, fixing errors. I couldn't believe how many there were. Christmas was spelled wrong, for Pete's sake. But finally, after hours of agonizing horror, it was ready to send back to Rachel for formatting—again. I was really excited about it because not only would the errors be fixed, but this version would have little crowns above the chapter titles, and Rachel revamped the cover for a fresh new look. It was better than ever!

I got the book back. It was beautiful. I re-published the book. I got my copy...

We Prewitt's enjoy the finer things in life.

Prewitt's. After all of that editing and scouring the manuscript for errors, I had missed the second word of the first page.

Thankfully, Rachel fixed it immediately. Unbelievable.

You would think that after that experience, I would have certainly gotten someone else to edit my books for me to keep this from happening again. You would be wrong. I still edit my own books, and while I am getting much better at it, I still have much improving to do. The books are cleaner typo-wise and grammatically as the series progresses, but to this day, you will still find Maggie's mother whaling instead of wailing at Maggie's father's funeral. At one point, Eve the Wise queen of all people, says "could care less" instead of "couldn't care less." Also, Atticus, when playing in the snow, is dressed for the great white *artic* instead of *arctic.*

But while these kinds of mistakes are throughout, it doesn't negate the fact that the story is a good one. And because it is mine, like my children are mine—God has purposely set me as the mother of Ryan and Anna, and He has set me as the author of *Brumbletide*—it is my favorite, like my children are my favorite. Other books are better, more successful, more well-written, but in my eyes, mine is the best because it is mine, and I am so grateful to God that He picked me to write it.

As of now, there are five published books in the series. I am currently writing the sixth. There will be seven.

Chapter 24
The Vine and the Branch

"Get up and go, Maggie. I am going to rescue them."
I stand up immediately and brighten. "Really? That's fantastic! Ugh, I was so
afraid I was going to have to do it."
"You will do it."

J. Reese Bradley, Brumbletide and the Changing of the Crowns

As far as now and going forward, I don't know much. My kids are eleven and seven, so I have no parenting advice since how they will turn out remains to be seen. I am in my second marriage and do not have much advice for you there either. In this world that is much different than the one I grew up in, I am taking the approach of talking with my kids immediately about whatever it is when it comes up. I have already had many conversations with both of my kids that I never had to have with my parents at their age. Again, I do not know if this will turn out for better or worse, but it is how I am doing it.

As for marriage, the best advice I can give you is to pass gas in front of your significant other as early in the relationship as possible. You will both be so glad you did, as marriage is hard enough without stomach discomfort.

But one thing I do know about how to live life is this way of the Vine and the branch.

"I am the true vine, and My Father is the keeper of the vineyard. He cuts off every branch in Me that bears no fruit, and every branch that does bear fruit, He prunes to make it even more fruitful. You are already clean because of the word I have spoken to you. Remain in Me, and I will remain in you. Just as no branch can bear fruit by itself unless it remains in the vine, neither can you bear fruit unless you remain in Me.

I am the vine and you are the branches. The one who remains in Me, and I in him, will bear much fruit. For apart from Me you can do nothing. If anyone does not remain in Me, he is like a branch that is thrown away and withers. Such branches are gathered up, thrown into the fire, and burned. If you remain in Me and My words remain in you, ask whatever you wish, and it will be done for you. This is to My Father's glory, that you bear much fruit, proving yourselves to be My disciples.

As the Father has loved Me, so have I loved you. Remain in My love. If you keep My commandments, you will remain in My love, just as I have kept My Father's commandments and remain in His love. I have told you these things so that My joy may be in you and your joy may be complete.

John 15:1-11

We live in a busy culture, and even if we are not busy, it doesn't seem like stopping what we are doing to read an ancient text is worthwhile, even if we say it is. Prayer, too, seems daunting. What do we say?

I didn't think prayer and especially Bible reading were worthwhile ways to spend much time either, and when I decided

I wanted Christianity to be a part of my life—because that is all I wanted from it—I wanted only sermons that would give me advice to add to the plans that I had already made for myself. I didn't need or want God's plans; I had my own. This is the wrong way to go about living life, even if the plans we make are good ones.

Martin Luther said, "I have so much to do that I shall spend the first three hours in prayer."

And that is the way to go about it. It will do us well to make Bible reading and prayer the rule, and as a result we should have try to make time for everything else. This is how God intended life with His creation to be. God, man, and woman ruling the world together. But apart from Him, we can do nothing! We must constantly have our eyes on the Lord, all the while that our hands are on the plow.

We all have a purpose that was planned for us before the beginning of time. God knew you then and crafted your purpose and gifts accordingly. Our gifts are the same before and after we are born again into the New Creation, but they will only be used in the way they were intended after our rebirth. If everything works together for the good of those who love God, then that means that even the work of those who do not love God works together for the good of those who love God. So, before the rebirth, your gifts are being worked together for good—just not your good.

An artist may be extremely talented at sculpting and spend his life chipping away at an extraordinary creation, all the while missing the eighth world wonder that it could have been *and* shining light into the darkness at the same time with God working through him.

A savvy businesswoman may have many successful business ventures under her belt, but if she would have slowed down and said, "Here it is, Lord, the gift you have given me. Do with it what you will. Lead me in the way I should go." Those businesses would be extraordinary, indeed.

Our gifts were given for a special reason, and they will have only been used for that reason when submitted to God for Him to establish them. The housewife with a passion for homemaking. The housewife with a passion for science. The housewife with a passion for the outdoors. The housewife with a passion for cooking. I repeat myself because the role of the housewife is so important. The restaurant chef, the musician, the lyricist, the speaker, the builder, the plumber, the doctor, the lawyer, the manager, the accountant—all talents and gifts were given by God for God. He has given us our specific gifts for His glory. And His glory is our good.

God gave Abraham a son in his old age, and that son—the gift—was given with a promise that he would become a great nation. But God then asked Abraham to sacrifice the gift to see if he loved the gift more than the Giver. Abraham laid Isaac down on the altar before God and was about to sacrifice his son because he not only feared God but trusted that He would fulfill His promise that He made to him. Hebrews says that Abraham knew that God could even raise the dead! But God did not require the sacrifice of Isaac.

> *But the angel of the LORD called to him from heaven and said, "Abraham, Abraham!" And he said, "Here I am."*
> *He said, "Do not lay your hand on the boy or do anything to him, for now I know that you fear God, seeing you have not withheld your son, your only son, from me."*
>
> *Genesis 22:11-12*

Like Abraham, we must lay our gifts on the altar for God to do with them what He will. And we must live our lives with our eyes on the Lord and our hands on the plow. No matter if we are rich or poor, young or old, educated or uneducated, we must cling to the Vine. Then, and only then, will we bear the Fruit of the Spirit, which is love, joy, peace, patience, kindness, goodness, gentleness, faithfulness, and self-control. And it is only when we cling to the Vine, living not of ourselves but as Christ's vessels, that we are the light and salt of the earth, illuminating and preserving that which is worthy. And it is only when we cling to the Vine, and only then, that our joy is complete.

Chapter 25
The Mountain

C.S. Lewis, *The Great Divorce*

Seven years into new life, I am living on the Vine by the grace of the Vine. Seven years out of bondage. Seven years without anxiety. Seven years without constantly seeing the world through a haze. Seven years of truly living.

As far as daily life now, along with Bible, prayer, church, and wifehood, I am in the season of mother and writer. I spend my days raising my kids and writing these books. I enjoy it because I want to be a good mother and I want to be a good author even though I am constantly messing things up. I try my best to be diligent in prayer and in reading my Bible and so far, I have been successful.

I never throw up after I eat. I still can't believe I'm on this side of it. I do still obsess about things sometimes, but not at all like I used to, and there is no fear behind them when I do have obsessions. I still fixate on numbers a lot even though I am not afraid of them. I still have dreams that I think are from God sometimes, and sometimes they scare me. But my life does not stop because of them, nor do my thoughts revolve around them.

I truly believe the dream of Ryan and the snake was supposed to stop my life the way it did so that I would finally come to read the Bible and know the Gospel. But here is an example of an obsession that is pretty harmless yet has affected my life quite a bit. Four years ago, on November 8th, 2019, I had a dream. I was in a green car and pulled up on a grassy hill where a crimson-red door was standing all by itself, with no walls or anything holding it up. Behind the door, in the short distance, was a massive, majestic mountain covered in trees. I got out of the car, and from the back floorboard, I took a brown paper bag with two bottles of wine and two muffins in it. I walked to the door, put my hand on the knob, and right before opening it, I woke up.

Those of you who have read *Brumbletide* know I have a version of this dream in the story. Well, I haven't been able to get away from that dream for four years.

In the year after the dream, in this order, my brother asked me to work for him, my pastor asked me to be on the team to start Discipleship at my church, I began homeschooling Ryan, and I published *Brumbletide and the Daughter of Eve*. I convinced myself that those four things were the four things in the bag in the dream and proceeded to work diligently at each of them daily for four years. Most importantly, I worked to share the Gospel in all four things because, in my mind, that would be "taking them through the Door."

I am convinced that the Door is Jesus and the Mountain is the Mountain of God. You have to go through Jesus to be with God.

But most likely, it is all my imagination.

Was this dream from God? Who knows? But it wasn't harmful to do these things the past four years, and, in fact, it was quite beneficial. The most important thing in "following" this dream is that I am not motivated to do these things out of fear that I will be punished if I do not do them. There is zero fear that if I do not work on the four things daily, God will judge me. That is not how God speaks, but it is how OCD speaks. I have no fear and, in fact, have asked God several times that if He doesn't want me working on these things, like in the case of the books, to please shut them down. So, with no fear involved and the fact that there is fruit being born from this "obsession," it is more a quirk than anything, and quirks are not bad.

I cannot end this book without discussing the elephant in the room. Now that I am not living in bondage to my fears, what happens if all of the things I feared *do* come true? What if Ryan does end up dying before me? What if I fall into bulimia again? Was it all a sham?

Who knows what the future holds? The world may come to an end in my lifetime. My kids may die young. Maybe I will fall into depression or anxiety or back into disordered eating. Almost certainly, I will do narcissistic things. Maybe I will never be a well-known author or have a house that isn't halfway in shambles all the time. Maybe I will live in Georgia for the rest of my life and will never see the rest of the world. Maybe I will get sick. Maybe I will die in my 40s. Maybe…

But while I do not want tragedy to befall me—I absolutely hated writing "Ryan" and "die" so many times in this book—I do not obsess about them or even worry about them happening, and that is God's doing. Because of the Gospel, I know that if these terrible things happen, it is not because I am being punished but that God has a plan that it is all part of. How will I react? I have no idea. I hope I would long for heaven all the more.

As for the non-tragedies, while I would like people to read what I write, when it comes to success, God has planted Moses's sentiment in my heart.

> *Then Moses said to him, "If your Presence does not go with us, do not send us up from here.*
>
> *Exodus 33:15*

Everything may take a turn for the worse, but if that is so, God has given me a seven-year run of seeing His goodness. Seven years of living a life I never thought I would get to live! Seven years where I came to know and love Him, seven years of peace and a sound mind. And if it all takes a turn for the worse, He is still good, even if I can't see it through the pain. I do not know the future, but God, in His word, promises to keep me in His hand, and He promises to bring to completion the work that He started in me. I rest in that. Godliness plus contentment is great gain, indeed. Come with me through the Door to the Mountain.

I have seen the goodness of the LORD in the land of the living.

Estranging Novum

Other works by J. Reese Bradley

Brumbletide
and the Daughter of Eve

Brumbletide
and the Changing of the Crowns

Brumbletide
and the Triad Champion

Brumbletide
and the Queen's Doctor's Story

Brumbletide
and the Rise of the Firebreather